BEDSIDE BOOK

- OF -

PSYCHOLOGY

FROM ANCIENT DREAM THERAPY TO ECOPSYCHOLOGY

- 125 -

Historic Events and Big
Ideas to Push the Limits
of Your Knowledge

WADE E. PICKREN

STERLING
New York

STERLING
New York

An Imprint of Sterling Publishing Co., Inc.

Text © 2014, 2021 Wade Pickren
Cover © 2021 Sterling Publishing Co., Inc.

ISBN 978-1-4549-4281-8 (print format)
ISBN 978-1-4549-4282-5 (e-book)

Distributed in Canada by Sterling Publishing Co., Inc.
C/o Canadian Manda Group, 664 Annette Street
Toronto, Ontario, Canada M6S 2C8
Distributed in the United Kingdom by GMC Distribution Services
Castle Place, 166 High Street, Lewes, East Sussex, England BN7 1XU
Distributed in Australia by NewSouth Books
University of New South Wales, Sydney, NSW 2052, Australia

For information about custom editions, special sales,
and premium and corporate purchases, please
contact Sterling Special Sales at 800-805-5489
or specialsales@sterlingpublishing.com.

Manufactured in Canada

2 4 6 8 10 9 7 5 3 1

www.sterlingpublishing.com

Interior design by Christine Heun
Cover design by Elizabeth Mihaltse Lindy
Picture credits—see page 266

Contents

Introduction

"Everyone in the twentieth century . . . became her or his own psychologist, able and willing to describe life in psychological terms."

—Roger Smith, *The Human Sciences*, 1997

THE GREAT MEMORY SCIENTIST Hermann Ebbinghaus is often quoted as saying that psychology has a long past, but a short history. Humans have indeed thought about many of the ideas and practices that we now call psychology for a very long time. For about the last 150 years, there has been an effort to develop the scientific study of those ideas. In addition to science, modern psychology is also a profession, with many practices designed to help people live better lives and cope with the demands of society. This duality of psychology makes it a rich and rewarding subject that reaches into every aspect of our lives today.

The Scope of Psychology

Psychologists study topics that are of great interest and usefulness in everyday life, such as children's development, decision-making, work, sleep, aging, and health and many other topics. Psychologists have also developed a variety of theories about the functioning of the mind, from Freud's energy model to the computer model of Nobel Prize winner Herbert Simon. Therapies designed to help people cope with psychological problems have become an important part of psychologists' work, as well.

Modern psychological science and practices developed most rapidly in Europe and North America, but the roots of both science and practice can be found throughout recorded history. As will become apparent in this book, thoughtful people from a variety of times and places have contributed to our understanding of ourselves. For thousands of years, psychological principles were closely linked to religion, philosophy, and medicine, and other systems of thought, including astrology and astronomy. In every civilization there have been people who wrote about the human spirit, about mind and behavior, and tried to understand disorders of the mind. Among people who were not educated or even literate, systems of thought linked to the body, such as palmistry, physiognomy, and phrenology became popular as a way to understand themselves and others.

The Bedside Book of Psychology is about psychological ideas and the people behind those ideas over the centuries. Human and animal psychology have fascinated some of the world's great thinkers and we will explore what they have said and written about it. For example, the American philosopher and psychologist William James once wrote a friend that "psychology is a damnable subject, and all that one may wish to know lies entirely outside it." James wrote this out of exasperation after spending twelve years writing what is considered one of the greatest books in the field, *The Principles of Psychology* (1890). Clearly, James did not reject psychology; he, in fact, continued to make significant contributions until his death in 1910. His comment may best be understood as reflecting the complexity of psychology. How can we ever understand something as varied as human thought and behavior?

In fact, psychology is one of the most complex of all scientific and professional fields. It often appears at first glance as just a matter of common sense, its truths intuitively accessible or a matter of common folk knowledge. Yet, as we look closer we see that what appeared on the surface as common sense is, in fact, a matter of deep knowledge rich in nuance and subtlety. An example from cognitive psychology may serve as an illustration. Two Israeli psychologists, Daniel Kahneman and Amos Tversky, wondered what might lead people to make decisions that were not rational or in their best interest. They found that when a person has to make a decision in a condition of uncertainty—for example, when asked whether more people die in plane crashes or automobile accidents—the person may rely on a mental shortcut or heuristic to help them decide. These shortcuts may be based on the ease with which an example comes to mind—the availability heuristic—or by assuming similarity where none exists—the representativeness heuristic. Kahneman and Tversky showed that human beings are not always and perhaps not even primarily rational in making decisions. Of course, Sigmund Freud had argued that humans are not creatures of reason almost a century before Kahneman and Tversky, although he based his arguments on very different evidence. In *The Bedside Book of Psychology*, we will encounter questions about rationality, emotionality, and their important consequences many times.

What about the multitude of human behaviors that are so important, not only for our personal survival, but for the survival of our species? Freud, as you may know, wrote extensively about human sexuality. He claimed that the most basic motivation in life is sex and that our personalities are shaped very early in life by how we resolve the tensions between pleasure and the dictates of society as embodied in our parents. Before and after Freud, people have theorized about the place of sex in human life and how to understand the powerful sexual urges that most humans feel. In some societies, sexuality is celebrated and open, while in others it is a taboo topic, at least in public. Recently, evolutionary psychologists have theorized that the template for male-female sexual attraction is based in our ancient evolutionary past. Other psychologists argue that sexual attraction is socially constructed and that what we see as desirable is shaped by the environment in which we live.

In today's world of ongoing crises such as the Covid-19 pandemic and climate change, people are concerned about their personal or psychological resources. Their concerns are often expressed in such questions as, How can I be a resilient person? or, Am I able to create and sustain healthy relationships that can help me be a happy and successful person? Human beings have sought answers for these and other questions for millennia. The signs of the zodiac created by various astrological systems from ancient Mesopotamia, Egypt, and medieval Islam were all attempts to understand oneself and others. Palmistry and numerology are also ancient strategies to understand, predict, and control human behavior. Among the ancient Greeks, the Pythagoreans and others developed a sophisticated philosophical system based on numbers and their relationships that were used to understand the world, including human behaviors. In fact, the human body has often been used as a way for people to understand themselves. Physiognomy is an old system for understanding human character by the shape of one's face, and phrenology offered explanations of character and abilities based on the shape and protrusions of the human skull. Similar body-based theories have continued to our own day, with such well-respected developmental psychologists as Jerome Kagan and Nathan Fox claiming that there are typical body differences between shy and non-shy children. In the twentieth century, psychologists developed other approaches that were based on responses to surveys and questionnaires. This allowed for statistical manipulation of the respondents' data and resulted in an apparently more scientific approach to personality theory. However, older theories, such as those of Sigmund Freud or Carl Jung, have retained great appeal to millions of people around the world. We will explore several landmark theories of human personality in *The Bedside Book of Psychology*.

You will find the rich variety of human experience described in *The Bedside Book of Psychology* intellectually exciting and stimulating. We will note the important discoveries and theories in many areas of psychology. Since psychology connects with almost every other domain of life on this planet, it will be difficult to touch on all of those connections. But you will find interesting, important, and sometimes humorous milestones here. What people have thought about human relationships from love to sex to friendship to hate are all represented in the book. So, too, important contributions to understanding human development from the womb to the tomb can be found in our volume. Work life is an important domain for each of us and psychologists have made many important contributions to its understanding. Personality and mental health/illness are often linked and we will see what key contributions have been made in these related areas. Psychology encompasses the brain and its relation to behavior. In the twenty-first century, people and governments around the world are learning how to respond and cope with viral pandemics such as the Covid-19 crisis that began in 2020, or with the changes created by the ongoing climate crisis. Psychology may be one of humanity's best resources for the challenges, large and small, that we all face.

Chronology

The Bedside Book of Psychology is organized according to the year associated with an entry. For very early contributions, the date may not be absolutely certain. In most cases, however, we can point to a particular date when a theory was proposed, a book was published, or an event occurred. When there is a matter of debate, I will use the date or period most commonly agreed on.

Theories and discoveries in psychology are among the most fascinating phenomena known to human beings. We remain of perpetual interest to ourselves. *The Bedside Book of Psychology* is intended to give you even more to wonder about yourself, your friends, and your world.

SHAMANISM

Henri Ellenberger (1905–93), Sudhir Kakar (b. 1938)

THE DISCOVERY IN ISRAEL of the 12,000-year-old remains of a prominent female, along with more than seventy tortoise shells, in a burial pit within a cave dates the practice of shamanism to at least 10,000 BCE. It is common in modern histories to discount the "medicine" practiced in preliterate or undeveloped societies. Historian of psychodynamic practice Henri Ellenberger and Indian psychoanalyst and historian Sudhir Kakar, however, have shown how those practices brought healing and relief, both psychological and physical, to the people in their communities.

Shamanic practices were the first psychotherapies, and they were successful because they were rooted in the worldview of their communities. Two examples will help us understand. Many preliterate societies thought that a person becomes ill when the soul leaves the body, perhaps because it was stolen. The work of the shaman is to find the soul and restore it to the body. In Siberia, the shaman may have to travel to the land of the spirits to find the soul. While there, the shaman may bargain with the spirits, offer gifts, or even fight with them for the soul, which he then restores to the body. In Latin America, a person who suffers from *susto* (Spanish for "fright") has lost his or her soul as a result of being frightened or under the spell of evil influences. The *curandero* may perform a public healing ceremony that involves the preparation of a special mixture of flowers or grain that is left in the patient's clothing at night. The *curandero* then marks a trail with the same mixture so that the spirit can find its way back to the person's body.

The connection between these shamanic practices and modern psychotherapy is in the restoration of what was lost to the patient. In our time, a person is said to be alienated or to have lost his mind; the work of the healer is to find ways to restore that which has been lost.

This nineteenth-century engraving depicts a Yakutian shaman (from the Russian region of Sakha) performing a ritual to invoke the spirits to cure a sick man.

SEE ALSO Jungian Psychology: Collective Unconscious and Psychological Growth (1913), Psychoanalysis: The Talking Cure (1899), Culture Determines What Counts as Mental Illness (1904)

BUDDHA'S
FOUR NOBLE TRUTHS

Siddhartha Gautama (c. 563–c. 483 BCE)

EXTANT ACCOUNTS OF THE BUDDHA'S LIFE in Ancient India indicate that he grew up amid great wealth and had a privileged and sheltered existence. While still a young man, Siddhartha Gautama was confronted with suffering in the world on three important occasions. On his first trip outside the palace where he lived, Siddhartha went to a nearby town and came upon an old man; he had never seen an elderly person before. On his second trip to the town he came upon a sick man, and on his third trip he came upon people carrying a corpse to its resting place. Lastly, he saw an ascetic meditating under a tree. These encounters affected him deeply and led to the realization that wealth and privilege offered little protection from suffering.

> Buddha taught that we must embrace the Four Noble Truths if we are to overcome suffering.

At around the age of twenty-nine, Gautama left his home and family and began the life of a religious wanderer. For six years he studied with spiritual teachers but found the rigors of asceticism and self-mortification to be ineffective in dealing with suffering; he realized that such practices could not lead to enlightenment.

Then, when he was about thirty-five, he decided to sit quietly under a tree and reflect on the human condition until he attained enlightenment.

Legend has it that while sitting thus under a fig tree, or Bodhi tree, he was enlightened and became the Buddha, seeing that what was required was the Middle Way—a life of discipline without the extremes of self-indulgence or self-mortification.

As the Buddha, he taught that there are three basic characteristics of existence: (1) everything is impermanent, and thus change is constant; (2) there is no self or immortal soul; and (3) suffering, or dissatisfaction, is at the core of existence. Buddha taught that we must embrace the Four Noble Truths if we are to overcome suffering. The first truth is that suffering exists, the second is that desire is the root of suffering, the third is that if we eliminate desire we can end suffering, and the fourth truth is that there is a Noble Eightfold Path, or Middle Way, that will lead to enlightenment.

Buddha and his followers' teachings over the centuries are an elaboration of how to follow the Middle Way. In contemporary life, Buddhist psychology has introduced meditation and mindfulness into everyday life and into psychotherapy. Buddhist psychology deals with insight, personal transformation, and deeper awareness of reality and holds great appeal for personal and social liberation.

SEE ALSO Mindfulness and Mind-Body Medicine (1993)

CONFUCIAN PSYCHOLOGY

Confucius (551–479 BCE)

KONG FUZI ("MASTER KONG"), known in English as Confucius, played many roles in his life: diplomat, teacher, and philosopher. Around 500 BCE, he also became an important political adviser. His teaching on the Way of Humanity provided a model for how to live, how to understand one's obligations, and how to treat others.

The five interrelated aspects of Confucianism are destiny, mind, ethics for ordinary people, self-cultivation, and ethics for scholars. Confucius stated simply that we all share the destiny of birth, aging, disease, and death, but we nevertheless have a responsibility to act morally in relation to our fellow humans. The Confucian model of mind has two aspects: a mind of discernment, which includes our cognitive abilities, and a mind of benevolence, which is our ethical mind or conscience.

Ethics for ordinary people asks each person to show benevolence or affection toward those who are close, and to act righteously, showing respect for each person, especially to those who have superior social rank; in doing so, the person will observe propriety and contribute to smooth social functioning. Benevolence, righteousness, and propriety make up the Way of Humanity, which is intended to reflect the Way of the Heavens. Through self-cultivation in the Way of Humanity, we develop into people of deep moral character and move toward attaining the three virtues of wisdom, benevolence, and courage.

Since the end of the Cultural Revolution in China in the mid-1970s, the discipline of psychology has grown rapidly, as indicated by its esteemed place in the Chinese Academy of Sciences. Chinese psychologists have built on the Confucian tradition to empirically demonstrate that the traits of interpersonal relatedness, holism, dialectical self, relationship harmony, and concern with face are unique expressions of the Chinese personality.

This illustration of Confucius appeared in the *Atlas général de la Chine . . .*, by Jean Baptiste Bourguignon d'Anville, c. 1790. The caption noted that Confucius was "the most famous philosopher of China."

SEE ALSO Sikolohiyang Pilipino (1975)

ASCLEPIUS AND
THE ART OF HEALING

ASCLEPIUS WAS AN IMPORTANT FIGURE in Greek mythology who became the god of healing and medicine. In some stories, he is a man, in others a god. His father was Apollo, also associated with healing, and his mother was the mortal Coronis; she died either in childbirth or by the devices of Apollo. Asclepius was raised and tutored by the centaur Chiron, wise and skilled in the arts of medicine, who passed on this knowledge to Asclepius.

Asclepius became knowledgeable in surgery and the uses of various drugs, potions, and healing incantations. He received from the goddess Athena a powerful potion made from the blood of the snake-haired Gorgons, whose appearance turned people to stone; the mixture had the power to heal or even bring the dead back to life, but it also could be a deadly poison.

With his great knowledge and skill, Asclepius became widely known and revered for his treatments. He took as his symbol the staff with an entwined serpent, which represents the duality of the physician's work—life and death, sickness and health. Around 350 BCE, his followers initiated the cult of Asclepius and established centers for treatment, called *asclepeia*.

Those who sought treatment in *asclepeia* underwent a period of purification, drank the waters of a sacred fountain, and then spent one or more nights sleeping in special clothing in an underground chamber. There, Asclepius would reveal the cure of the illness, provide an oracular dream, or sometimes the dream itself would bring healing.

The cult of Asclepius indicates the historic connection between spirituality, religion, and medicine. The art of healing was considered sacred, and the practices were secret, passed from father to son. Asclepian medicine, with its dream therapy, also represents an early form of psychological treatment and thus is an important precursor to modern psychological medicine.

Asklepios und Hygieia.

A nineteenth-century engraving of a Roman statue of Asclepius, with his serpentine staff, and Hygieia, Asclepius's daughter and the goddess of hygiene.

SEE ALSO Jungian Psychology: Collective Unconscious and Psychological Growth (1913), Mindfulness and Mind-Body Medicine (1993)

BHAGAVAD GITA

HINDUISM IS THE NAME given by the British to a set of diverse but related religious beliefs and practices on the subcontinent of India. Thus Hindu psychology is not a discipline in the Western sense but rather a mixture of psychological principles and practices grounded in the traditions known as Hinduism.

This nineteenth-century chromolithograph depicts an important scene from the Mahābhārata: the prince Arjuna requests instruction from Krishna and receives the Bhagavad Gita.

There are several ancient texts that form the foundation of Hinduism: the Vedas, the Upanishads, and the Purānas. More "recent" texts include the Mahābhārata, from about the second century BCE. One of the principal epics, or stories, within the Mahābhārata is the Bhagavad Gita. For sake of simplicity, a few principles from these texts are mentioned here, but they by no means incorporate the richness of Hindu thinking about mind, self, and relationships.

Three *gunas*, or principles, work together to create all that occurs in the universe. The gunas are *tamas* (inertia), *rajas* (activity), and *sattva* (clarity, or light). All three are necessary, but *sattva* is considered the spiritual element, and it is desirable to cultivate this *guna* while maintaining an equilibrium, allowing all three to work together. The intent through practice of these principles—Yoga—is to calm the mind so that self-realization or awareness can occur. When we learn self-control, right action, and practice Yoga, we can change our consciousness so that unhelpful thoughts and habits are transformed into positive and constructive thoughts and actions. There are multiple Yogas, each with a particular emphasis, such as action, sacred chanting, devotion, or knowledge.

In Western terms, these practices are meant to lead to psychological growth, which, according to Hinduism, occurs throughout four life stages: student, householder, forest dweller, and renunciant. Each stage has its own lessons that a person must learn on the way to self-realization. It is common for a person to seek out a guru for guidance, instruction, and especially self-development.

SEE ALSO Mindfulness and Mind-Body Medicine (1993)

HUMORAL THEORY

Hippocrates (c. 460–370 BCE), Galen (131–c. 200 CE)

HUMORAL THEORY is a theory of balance and imbalance in relation to health and personality. It shares much with other balance theories, such as traditional Chinese medicine, Ayurvedic medicine, and Unani. Humoral theory was first articulated around the fourth century BCE by the Greek physician Hippocrates, who proposed that a balance of four basic fluids (blood, phlegm, yellow bile, and black bile) was vital for healthy bodies. The Roman physician, surgeon, and philosopher Galen incorporated and extended Hippocratic theory to describe human personality in his dissertation *De temperamentis* (c. 160 CE). A *sanguine* (confident, cheerful) personality is one in which blood is the dominant humor, while the *phlegmatic* personality is calm and unemotional. The *choleric* personality is angry, reflecting the hot and dry characteristics of yellow bile. Finally, the *melancholic* personality is a result of the dominance of black bile and is characterized as sad and gloomy. The ideal personality resulted from a balanced mix of these humors.

> Humoral and other balance theories assumed physical health and individual personality were connected as part of the greater circle of life.

For Hippocrates, Galen, and those who followed, humoral and other balance theories assumed physical health and individual personality were connected as part of the greater circle of life that also incorporated the stars and planets, the political sphere, community life, diet, and climate. All these facets had important implications for any individual's health and fortune. Since physical and mental disease were thought to be a result of humoral imbalance, a physician was expected to know the patient intimately enough to provide individualized treatment, taking into account the astrological, climatological, social, and temperamental factors that might upset the natural humoral balance of the patient.

Humoral theory has persisted into our own time, although the term *temperament* is preferred. Theories of personality developed by Carl Jung owed a great deal to the humoral tradition, especially in the Myers-Briggs Type Indicator, the widely used test based on Jung's work. The advent of modern biomedicine discounted the humoral approach, but by the late twentieth century the need to recognize psychological factors was once again thought vital to appropriate health care.

SEE ALSO Jungian Psychology: Collective Unconscious and Psychological Growth (1913), Thematic Apperception Test: Our Stories and Our Personality (1935)

AVICENNA AND THE FIRST ISLAMIC PSYCHOLOGY

Avicenna (980–1037)

ABŪ ʿALĪ AL-HUSAYN IBN ʿABD ALLĀH IBN SĪNĀ, known in the West as Avicenna, was perhaps the most important philosopher of the Islamic tradition as well as an accomplished physician. He was a prolific author whose writings on a range of critical topics in metaphysics, ontology, epistemology, and psychology became a major influence in Western philosophy through his influence on Thomas Aquinas. Avicenna's massive medical work, the *Canon of Medicine*, completed in 1025, was the standard medical reference work in Europe and in the Arab world until at least the seventeenth century.

Avicenna, the son of a Persian tax collector, demonstrated a formidable memory and intellect at a very early age. By the age of sixteen he was a practicing physician. Over the course of his life, he served as a judge, a teacher, a political administrator, and as a royal physician and vizier. Given how busy he was, one may wonder how he managed to be so productive as a scholar.

In psychology, Avicenna developed the "floating man" thought experiment as a means to explore self-awareness. The experiment asks us to imagine we are floating in the air without any contact with our senses; Avicenna argues that we would still know we exist. Such self-consciousness, he concludes, indicates that the soul, or self, is separate from the body.

Book 1 of the *Canon of Medicine* addresses the interplay between mind and body in health. In it, Avicenna adapts the old notion of the four humors and posits four temperaments that interact with them. Mental and emotional habits influence our physical health, he argues, but the body also influences our mind and emotions. Thus exercise will have a beneficial effect on our mental and emotional health. In this, he anticipated some of the tenets of modern health psychology.

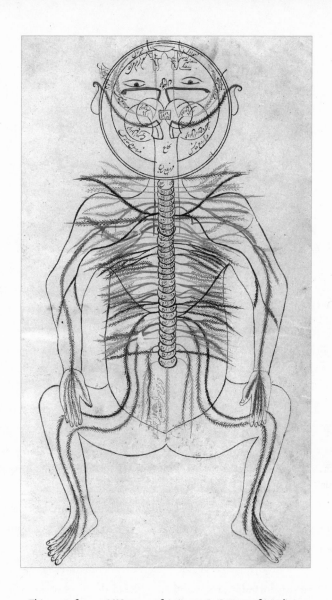

This page from a 1632 copy of Avicenna's *Canon of Medicine* describes the peripheral nervous system.

SEE ALSO Psychoneuroimmunology (1975), Mindfulness and Mind-Body Medicine (1993)

PROTESTANTISM AND THE PSYCHOLOGICAL SELF

Martin Luther (1483–1546)

WHEN THE GERMAN CATHOLIC MONK Martin Luther wrote his *Ninety-Five Theses* in 1517, condemning the practices of the Catholic Church, he set into motion momentous changes—not only in religious practices but also in the understanding of human identity. Each person now stood alone before God, each person's justification was through faith alone, and one's relationship with the deity was defined in personal terms. By contrast, salvation, in the Catholic faith, was mediated by the church; thus the individual identity was submerged in the collective identity of church membership.

While Luther's immediate aim was to challenge what he considered false practices by the church, the consequences of his actions spread far beyond the church and matters of religion. The implications of the Reformation contributed to a new sense of self. The emergent Protestant faith demanded that its followers focus on their inner lives and devote themselves to spiritual practices. The emphasis on a personal, private relationship with God facilitated a need to pay attention to one's thoughts and emotions, thus increasing a sense of subjectivity. The practices of everyday life attained a new importance, as one's faith was manifested as much in the way one conducted business and attended to the tasks of daily living as in the number of times one attended church. New tools, such as conduct books and diaries, were introduced to help Christians maintain their personal relationships with God.

The most popular devotional aid was the conduct book, which was filled with maxims and proverbs meant to guide spiritual reflection and help each person judge his or her own spiritual progress. Both conduct books and diaries were ways to help the believer pay careful attention to the inner life and so enhance self-control of sinful thoughts and impulses. The focus on the inner life became a crucial building block of the modern sense of the private self and its subjectivity, which helped pave the way to modern psychology and its emphasis on the private self.

> The emphasis on a personal, private relationship with God facilitated a need to pay attention to one's thoughts and emotions.

SEE ALSO Montaigne's *Essays* (1580), Tabula Rasa: The Psychology of Experience (1690)

MONTAIGNE'S *ESSAYS*

Michel de Montaigne (1533–92)

"I AM MYSELF THE SUBJECT of my book," declared the French philosopher Michel de Montaigne in the introduction to his collection of essays. At the time that Montaigne wrote this, it was an unusual declaration to make. Most public writing was about theological or scientific subjects, or some mixture of the two. But Montaigne made his life the topic—a subject, he declared, "in regard to which I am the most learned man alive." In writing this way, Montaigne foreshadowed our modern sense of self and personal identity.

Modern psychology takes for granted a personal sense of individuality and a private, interior life. This has not always been the case. Our sense of self, as a personal "I" at the center of our own worlds, has slowly developed through changes in philosophy, medicine, religion, and everyday practices. Published in 1580, Montaigne's *Essais* was an important early contributor to this sense of self.

The essay as a form of writing was invented by Montaigne. It was an ideal genre in which to account for his experience. Why invent a new form? Montaigne was educated as a lawyer, but retired from practice when he was only thirty-eight years old. He lived at a time of intense conflict between Catholics and the new Protestant faith. Nations went to war over matters of religion, and religious persecution was present everywhere. The claims for knowledge and certainty based on religion, Montaigne concluded, only led to more conflict and bloodshed, and he became skeptical of governments, customs, and the supposed superiority of humans over animals. Montaigne pointed out that human experience is always changing; thus knowledge is always changing, too.

Montaigne developed the essay as a way to account for his changing experience. In giving his account, he made it possible for others to think of their own individual experiences as valid ways of making sense of the world.

OPPOSITE: Michel de Montaigne is depicted on this frontispiece to a seventeenth-century London edition of his *Essays*.

SEE ALSO Descartes on Mind and Body (1637), Tabula Rasa: The Psychology of Experience (1690)

DESCARTES ON MIND AND BODY

René Descartes (1596–1650)

IN THE SEVENTEENTH CENTURY, a new understanding of the natural world placed humans and their abilities within a framework of natural law. The writings of the French philosopher René Descartes, especially *Discourse on the Method* (1637), became a resource for these efforts.

Descartes sought to remain true to the Catholic Church while searching for a natural understanding of the human mind and body. Catholicism held that the mind is under the direct influence of God; thus the soul is distinct from the body and cannot be explained as only part of nature. To avoid conflict with the church, Descartes proposed a mind-body dualism in which some mental functions could be considered properties of the body rather than the soul. Claiming that memory, perception, imagination, dreaming, and feelings were bodily processes meant that they could be investigated and understood by humans as part of the natural order.

Descartes drew on earlier discoveries in medicine, such as William Harvey's description of the heart as a pump (1628), and from the work of craftsmen who created objects that worked mechanically, such as those in the royal gardens outside Paris. There, hydraulic pressure activated statues when visitors stepped on hidden plates, making it seem as if they moved on their own. Descartes used the principle of mechanical movement as a model for how we can understand memory, dreaming, and other mental acts without relying on divine Providence. He theorized that the mind and body interact via the brain's pineal gland, which receives bodily impressions and transmits movement to the body. This preserved the soul as the seat of reason and kept it as the special province of divine influence.

Descartes's approach fit with both the teachings of the Catholic Church and the new mechanical philosophy. In articulating this division between mind and body, he left a legacy that helped later thinkers consider humans part of the natural, rather than supernatural, order.

Grotto d'Orphée, an engraving by Abraham Bosse, c. 1620s, illustrating one of the automatons Descartes likely saw in the French royal gardens at the Château de Saint-Germain-en-Laye. The automaton statue of Orpheus would play his lyre while the animals and trees in the grotto would lean in to listen.

SEE ALSO Tabula Rasa: The Psychology of Experience (1690)

1664

CEREBRI ANATOME:
ON THE BRAIN
AND BEHAVIOR

Thomas Willis (1621–75)

IN *CEREBRI ANATOME* ("Anatomy of the Brain"), physician and anatomist Thomas Willis laid much of the foundation of modern neurology and psychiatry, coining the term *neurologie* in the volume. He sought, as he wrote to a friend, "to unlock the secret places of Man's Mind." The writings of Willis on the brain in both its normal and pathological state were immensely influential in his own time and helped redirect the study of the brain in the direction of our current understanding. For example, within a year of its publication in English in 1664, *Cerebri Anatome* went through four Latin editions, and five more editions followed over the next few years. The book was actually a collaboration between Willis and several of his colleagues, including the noted architect and artist Sir Christopher Wren, who provided the engravings for the volume.

> Willis viewed the brain as "the chief seat of the Rational Soul in a man . . . and as the chief mover in the animal Machine."

Willis was educated at Christ Church, Oxford, and remained in Oxford until his move to London in 1667. He was intimately involved with the new experimental philosophy that was emerging then. Willis's specialty was chemistry and the blood; but about 1660, his interests shifted to neuroanatomy and neurology.

As he followed his new interests, Willis brought to them the same careful observation and vast learning that had marked his career to date. Willis viewed the brain as "the chief seat of the Rational Soul in a man ... and as the chief mover in the animal Machine," and engaged Christopher Wren and others to work with him on what would become *Cerebri Anatome*. In the book, he used the format of comparative anatomy that had been pioneered by physician and anatomist William Harvey in his work on the circulation of blood. Willis used examples from both nonhuman vertebrates and invertebrates to inform his argument about the brain's anatomy and related functions. He also used patient case histories and postmortem anatomies to support his conclusions. In addition to neuroanatomy, the book also described and illustrated the cranial, spinal, and autonomic nerves.

Together with *Pathologiae Cerebri* (1667), which extended his analysis to brain disorders, *Cerebri Anatome* offered the first comprehensive account of the brain and nervous system in Europe.

SEE ALSO Descartes on Mind and Body (1637), Where Brain Functions Are Localized (1861), Mirror Neurons (1992)

TABULA RASA:
THE PSYCHOLOGY OF EXPERIENCE

John Locke (1632–1704)

A stipple engraving of John Locke by Louis Lecoeur, 1800.

HOW DO WE GAIN KNOWLEDGE? For the English philosopher John Locke, this was a fundamental question for which the answer was human experience. In his major work, *An Essay Concerning Human Understanding* (1690), Locke rejected the notion of innate ideas and argued that all ideas come through experience. Thus, at birth the human mind is a tabula rasa (Latin for "blank slate") on which sensory experiences are inscribed, and its contents are those ideas that come from experiences. Knowledge, then, is a matter of the mind gathering experiences and ideas from the material world. Locke proposed a way in which we could understand how ideas could move from simple to complex through association. In doing so, he laid the foundation for empirical philosophy and, much later, the new science of psychology.

What motivated Locke to propose such a new and radical approach? When he was only ten years old, religious and political differences between the king and Parliament led to civil war, and for nearly twenty years daily life was dangerous and full of conflict. He wanted to find a better basis for social life, and he thought he could help create conflict-free society by encouraging people to form clear and distinct ideas that were not based in political or religious excesses.

Why is this important for us today? In addition to sparking a nature vs. nurture debate that extends to this day, Locke's idea helped make it possible to think about human behavior in terms of natural law rather than divine intervention, ultimately making a science of psychology possible.

SEE ALSO Nature vs. Nurture (1874), Stanford Prison Experiment (1970)

ROUSSEAU'S NATURAL CHILD

Jean-Jacques Rousseau (1712–78)

THE SWISS-BORN FRENCH PHILOSOPHER Jean-Jacques Rousseau drew upon a variety of sources, including travelers' reports from the Americas, to imagine the human condition prior to society. He thought that humans lived in noble simplicity in that earlier state: the natural child is born good and corrupted by society. He asked, "What type of misery there can be for a free being whose heart is at peace and whose body is healthy?" For Rousseau, human behavior is best guided by our emotions rather than by reason. In this, he is a forerunner of romanticism, with its emphasis on subjectivity.

The emphasis on an original human state of goodness led Rousseau to propose in *The Social Contract, or Principles of Political Right* (1762) that although humans are oriented to their own well-being, they also do not wish to see their fellows suffer. Social life is thus possible because of sentiment or fellow feeling, even though social life does not accord with the freedom of the individual.

Because we are born good but must live in society, Rousseau argued that education was the only route to minimize corrupting social influence and perfect our natures. Thus he became an advocate of developmentally appropriate education for children, rather than one that treated them as little adults. In his novel *Émile, or On Education* (1762), Rousseau divided human development into three stages, each with unique age-related characteristics. In doing so, Rousseau rejected the educational practices of his day with their emphasis on rote learning and argued instead for education based on the natural curiosity of the child. In this approach, education stimulates the mental and moral development of the child.

Rousseau's educational model is clearly psychological. His ideas influenced the nineteenth-century educational psychologies of Johann Pestalozzi and Friedrich Froebel and, through them, the innovative twentieth-century educational psychologies of Lev Vygotsky and Jerome Bruner.

A nineteenth-century lithographic portrait of Jean-Jacques Rousseau.

SEE ALSO Nature vs. Nurture (1874), Zone of Proximal Development (1934)

MESMERISM

Franz Anton Mesmer (1734–1805)

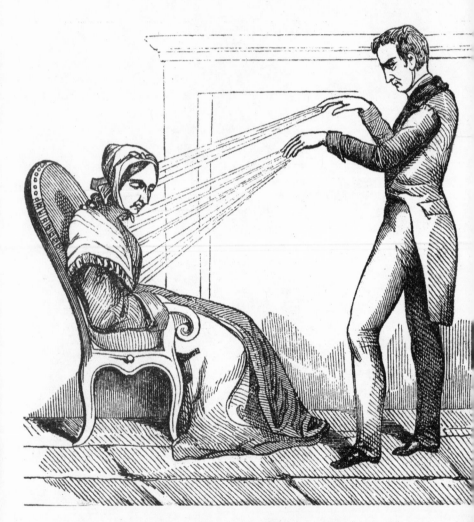

A mesmerist uses animal magnetism on a seated
female patient in this engraving, c. 1845.

LIKE OTHER THEORISTS OF HIS ERA, the German physician Franz Mesmer accepted the idea that the stars and the planets were constantly influencing human life, including a person's health. In his doctoral dissertation, written in 1766, Mesmer suggested that illness was a result of adverse planetary influence on the fluids in the human body and that healing was a matter of restoring this balance through what he called *animal magnetism.*

Over time, Mesmer refined his treatment techniques. He began by asking patients to handle iron bars that had been magnetized. As his renown grew, he believed that he could use his own animal magnetism to magnetize any object—plant, book, cloth, and so on—and these items could work, even at a distance, to restore magnetic equilibrium within his patients. Later in his career, Mesmer believed that his touch or a glance from him could restore patients' balance and bring healing.

After Mesmer was discredited in Vienna over his treatment of a talented young blind girl, he arrived in Paris in 1777. Soon he was treating wealthy ladies, including Marie Antoinette. There he introduced group treatment in a special room, where music played softly and seated patients held magnetized iron rods. Mesmer, clothed in royal purple, strode into the room and lightly touched the patients, usually provoking cries, convulsions, and even fainting. Many patients reported that they were cured by this treatment. Once again, Mesmer was rejected by the medical establishment, this time after a royal commission (which included Benjamin Franklin, then ambassador to France) concluded that any effects were due solely to his patients' imaginations.

Although Mesmer was discredited, his ideas lived on, undergoing many refinements over the nineteenth century with two very important results. First, the practice of hypnotism grew out of mesmerism. Second, Mesmer's work led to new theories about the unconscious and prepared the way for Freud's psychoanalysis.

SEE ALSO Phrenology (1832), Psychoanalysis: The Talking Cure (1899)

PHRENOLOGY

Franz Joseph Gall (1758–1828), Johann Spurzheim (1776–1832), Orson Fowler (1809–87), Lorenzo Fowler (1811–96), Samuel Wells (1820–75)

THE VIENNESE PHYSICIAN FRANZ JOSEPH GALL developed a method of relating the bumps and protrusions of the skull to underlying brain structure; this method was soon termed *phrenology*. In 1832, Gall's student Johann Spurzheim brought phrenology to America, where it became immensely popular during an era of great interest in self-improvement. The public accepted and believed that personality and character could not only be studied scientifically but that the application of such study could lead to personal improvement.

A pair of enterprising brothers was particularly successful in capitalizing on the popular appeal of phrenology in America. The Fowler brothers, Orson and Lorenzo, along with their brother-in-law Samuel Wells, opened phrenological clinics in New York, Boston, and Philadelphia in the late 1830s. The purpose of the clinics was to give phrenological examinations, or readings, often in response to specific requests from clients; for example, parents might want insight into their children's behavior problems, or engaged couples might want to assess their compatibility. Traveling phrenologists also toured the country, announcing their circuit in advance of their arrival and renting space to deliver readings to eager customers.

The Fowlers and other trained phrenologists provided individualized advice manuals and eventually published a range of what we would now consider self-help books. Titles included *Phrenology and Physiology Explained and Applied to Education and Self-Improvement*, *The Phrenological Self-Instructor*, and *How to Read Character: A New Illustrated Handbook of Phrenology and Physiognomy*. At one point there were even plans for a phrenological vending machine that would provide character analysis through a self-administered test on a coin-operated machine!

Despite the enormous popular appeal of phrenology and the efforts of the Fowlers to establish its professional legitimacy, its scientific validity was criticized consistently. However, in numerous ways, phrenology prepared Americans for the emergence of clinical psychology, with its variety of tests and therapies to help people understand and improve their lives.

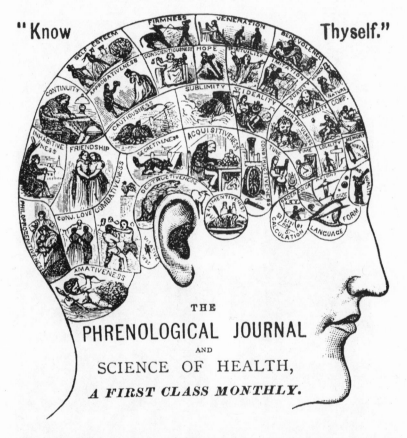

Phrenology chart from a nineteenth-century edition of the *Phrenological Journal*.

SEE ALSO Where Brain Functions Are Localized (1861), Somatotypes: Does Body Shape Reflect Our Personality? (1925)

FECHNER AND THE
JUST-NOTICEABLE DIFFERENCE (JND)

Ernst Weber (1795–1878), Gustav Fechner (1801–78)

German philosopher and psychologist Gustav Fechner, c. 1870.

MANY SCHOLARS IN THE EIGHTEENTH and nineteenth centuries believed that it was not possible to scientifically study the mind, in part because mental processes could not be described in mathematical terms.

German physiologist Ernst Weber's study of touch, first published in 1834, led to research on the human ability to perceive differences in sensation. Research on detecting variations in weight and temperature led him to conclude that such distinctions could be described lawfully, or mathematically; he found that the second, comparative weight must be heavier by a proportion of the original, not by an absolute amount, in order to make an accurate discrimination. In the case of each sensory modality—touch, light, sound, and so on—the amount necessary to detect a difference was proportional to the original stimulus. Weber calculated the proportions and established what he called the just-noticeable difference, or JND, for each sensory discrimination. For example, the just-noticeable difference for weight discrimination was always an amount equal to one-thirtieth of the heavier weight.

In 1850, German philosopher and psychologist Gustav Fechner empirically demonstrated a lawful relationship between the physical and psychological worlds. His experimental approach to this problem came to be known as psychophysics. Building on Weber's work on the JND, Fechner reasoned that if the JND was a constant fraction for each of the senses, then it could stand as a unit of measurement representing the subjectively experienced intensity of a stimulus. By starting with the lowest intensity of a stimulus that could be perceived and then plotting each successive JND, Fechner discovered a mathematical law that allowed him to describe and predict the relationship between the physical world and our subjective experience of that world.

Weber and Fechner proved that psychological phenomena could be described quantitatively.

SEE ALSO Psychology Becomes a Science (1874)

THE FIRST THINKING MACHINE

Charles Babbage (1791–1871), Ada, Countess of Lovelace (1815–52)

IN 1747, THE FRENCH PHYSICIAN and provocateur Julien Offray de La Mettrie published his book *L'homme machine* (*Man, a Machine*) and created an outrage. But almost a century later, the British polymath Charles Babbage designed a machine that could "think." He called his machine the Analytical Engine. In doing so, Babbage prefigured work on cognition, computers, and artificial intelligence in the mid-twentieth century.

> [Lovelace] cautioned . . . against the possibility that machines were capable of true creativity.

Babbage designed the device in the hope that machines could improve on human calculation. His first machine, the Difference Engine, was intended to calculate and print arithmetical tables automatically by using the principle of finite differences.

Later, Babbage designed a complex machine that could perform general computation, and it is this that makes him a pioneer of modern computing. The Analytical Engine was designed to use punched cards to control a mechanical calculator that could, in turn, use the input of prior computations. Babbage continued to tinker with his design until his death.

Ada Lovelace (as she is commonly known) was the daughter of the poet Lord Byron. A skilled mathematician, she struck up a friendship with Babbage. Her most important contribution to modern computing was her notes on a lecture given by an Italian engineer, Luigi Menabrea, concerning the Analytical Engine. In her notes, published in 1843, she explored the potential of the machine to operate not just on numbers but on any material that could be represented in an abstract form, such as musical pitch. She then surmised that it might be possible for the machine to compose, for example, elaborate pieces of music. She cautioned, however, against the possibility that machines were capable of true creativity; she claimed they can only accomplish what they are programmed to do. This became known as the "Lovelace objection."

Certainly, the Analytical Engine had some of the characteristics of the modern computer, such as programmability, a memory store, and a central processor. While never completed, Babbage's machine foreshadowed the modern computer and served as an inspiration for later scientists. Aspects of Babbage's work also anticipated modern cognitve science and artificial intelligence studies.

SEE ALSO Turing Machine (1937), Cybernetics, Computers, and the Beginning of Cognitive Science (1943)

THE CURIOUS CASE
OF PHINEAS GAGE

Phineas Gage (1823–60)

IN THE DAYS WHEN AMERICA'S network of railroads was growing quickly, an accidental explosion gave new insight into the link between an individual's brain and his or her personality. In 1848, Phineas Gage, a construction foreman on the Rutland and Burlington Railroad, was laying new track near Cavendish, Vermont. When he dropped the tamping iron for the dynamite by accident, it struck a spark and set off some nearby blasting powder. The explosion drove the tamping iron—some three feet, seven inches long—back through his skull, and it landed nearly one hundred feet away. The rod had passed through the front part of his brain and destroyed large parts of the frontal cortex, which is associated with behavior, motor skills, and problem solving. Gage also lost vision in his left eye.

Despite the severity of the injury, Gage survived. Remarkably, he did not lose consciousness immediately and was able to walk up the stairs to his hotel room. After his injury was cleaned, he said that he expected to return to work within a few days. His condition temporarily deteriorated, however, so he remained in bed. After recuperating at home in New Hampshire, he tried but was unable to return to his old job; instead, he worked in a stable

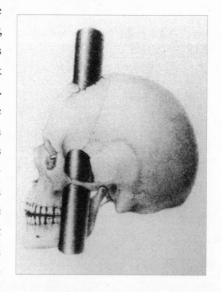

before moving to Chile, where he stayed for eight years. Gage developed epilepsy, and, nearing death, he returned to the United States.

The reason that Gage was unable to go back to his former job was that his personality had changed. In his position as foreman, Gage had been stable, reliable, and steady in his temperament. After his recovery, he was impulsive, childish, and given to displays of anger; it was also obvious that his intelligence had been compromised. Gage's terrible accident was the first clear indication of the close link between the frontal cortex and personality.

OPPOSITE: A lithograph of Gage's skull showing the iron bar protruding.

RIGHT: A cabinet-card portrait of brain-injury survivor Phineas Gage shown holding the tamping iron that injured him.

SEE ALSO Where Brain Functions Are Localized (1861), Right Brain, Left Brain (1962)

BIPOLAR DISORDER
AND CREATIVITY

Jean-Pierre Falret (1794–1870),
Emil Kraepelin (1856–1926)

THE OBSERVATION THAT MOOD STATES may swing back and forth rather freely for some people has been made for centuries; the scholar Robert Burton described it in *The Anatomy of Melancholy* (1621). Jean-Pierre Falret, a French physician at Hôpital de la Salpêtrière, used the term *la folie circulaire* ("circular insanity") to describe this vacillation in his patients, and in 1893, Emil Kraepelin, psychiatrist and founder of the modern classification schemes of mental disorders, rechristened "circular insanity" as manic-depressive psychosis. The fifth edition of the American Psychiatric Association's *Diagnostic and Statistical Manual of Mental Disorders*, or the DSM-5, labels these symptoms as bipolar disorder.

As these various labels indicate, the diagnosis includes the symptoms of depression and mania. In fact, the person may primarily exhibit depression, but if there's been one episode of mania, then the diagnosis is bipolar disorder. It is thought that a person suffering from manic depression will have recurring episodes once it begins.

While the depression side of the disorder is not hard to understand, what does *mania* refer to? The symptoms of mania are typically extreme, usually representing a break with reality, or psychosis. The mood may be elevated, even euphoric, and to achieve a definitive diagnosis the episode must last for at least a week. In some cases, the person is easily irritated and may become violent. Among the symptoms are extreme goal-directed activity and such rapidity of thought that it can be described as a flight of ideas; often there is a dramatically reduced need for sleep. In some cases, the person may experience delusions of grandeur.

Historically, there has been an association of creativity with manic depression. Prominent musicians, painters, poets, architects, and writers have been among those who have experienced the disorder. Many of them reported that their greatest and most intense moments of creativity occurred while they were in a manic state. The poet Lord Byron, the writer Virginia Woolf, the singer Rosemary Clooney, and many other artists are known to have suffered from the disorder.

> Prominent musicians, painters, poets, architects, and writers have been among those who have experienced the disorder.

SEE ALSO Bleuler Initiates the Modern Study of the Schizophrenias (1908)

·DARWIN'S
ON THE
ORIGIN OF SPECIES

Charles Darwin (1809–82)

IN SEPTEMBER OF 1831, Charles Darwin was interviewed by Captain Robert FitzRoy of the HMS *Beagle* for the position of gentleman companion on a two-year voyage for the purpose of mapping the coast of South America. But instead of two years, the *Beagle* sailed for more than twice that long on what became a trip around the world. Darwin, as the naturalist on board, busied himself collecting specimens and making careful observations throughout the trip. He filled a large scientific diary with thousands of geological and zoological data.

> [Darwin] settled on a theory of gradual evolutionary change by natural selection.

The *Beagle* docked at Falmouth, England, on October 2, 1836, nearly five years after it left Plymouth Sound. Darwin spent the next several years carefully considering his data and pondering questions about whether and how species change. Drawing on a range of sources, he eventually settled on a theory of gradual evolutionary change by natural selection.

He shared his theory only with a few close friends—until 1858, when he became aware of a very similar theory that had been developed by the British naturalist Alfred Russel Wallace. Fearing that he would not be credited for his years of painstakingly developing his theory, Darwin published his ideas in *On the Origin of Species* in 1859. Although almost all of his examples were drawn from observation of animals, Darwin included humans and mental life in his theorizing from the beginning. Darwin made four important contributions to the development of psychology.

First, he presented evidence that human beings are part of nature; thus we, like all other forms of life, are subject to the laws of nature.

Second, Darwin's approach made the function of a trait or ability an important aspect of its definition—that is, what does a particular trait or ability do for us? How does it aid survival?

Third, Darwin's theory suggested that human abilities could be compared fruitfully with those of other animals (what we call comparative psychology), and that this comparison aids our understanding of the development of human beings—a field that later came to be called developmental psychology.

Finally, his emphasis on the role of natural selection in human variability laid the foundation for a psychology of individual differences, which, in the United States, has had its greatest success as an instrument of social management.

SEE ALSO James's *The Principles of Psychology* (1890), Variability Hypothesis: Gender and Genius (1914)

MIND-CURE

Phineas P. Quimby (1802–66)

A NEW SELF-HELP MOVEMENT began in the late 1800s that brought together a variety of practices and beliefs about how to be healthy. It was called New Thought, or Mind-Cure.

The movement's founding father was Phineas P. Quimby, a clockmaker turned mesmerist turned healer. In 1859, Quimby settled in Portland, Maine, where he wrote and taught about the important connections among mind, behavior, and health. In Quimby's system of psychological healing, an intense rapport was developed with the patient, allowing the healer to see the false belief (about disease) that was the true cause of the illness. Treatment consisted of correcting the false belief, and health could be maintained through right thinking. This was one of the first psychological therapies.

Quimby's system was influential and appealed to people across the social and educational spectrum. Mary Baker Eddy, a former patient of Quimby's,

founded Christian Science in 1866, and by the early 1900s there was a growing number of women and men who developed Mind-Cure approaches influenced by Quimby. Many of these practitioners were loosely organized under the name of New Thought, and their appeal was wide. Some New Thought volumes sold hundreds of thousands or even millions of copies.

The American psychologist William James called this movement the "religion of healthy-mindedness." Clearly, millions of Americans believed in the importance of the mind-body connection in health and disease. For many, such belief was combined with special diets—vegetarianism, fruitarianism, herbalism—and exercise in order to maximize health and mental functioning. The healthy person was one who was fit in body, mind, and spirit.

Over the course of the twentieth century, this willingness to believe in the importance of

the mind-body connection was manifested in new scientific approaches, including psychosomatic medicine, health psychology, and psychoneuroendocrinology, along with continuing interest in herbs, diet, and exercise.

OPPOSITE: A bookplate from the First Church of Divine Science in Cleveland, Ohio, dated to the early twentieth century.

ABOVE: A lithograph of Phineas P. Quimby. Mary Baker Eddy was one of Quimby's disciples and extrapolated the principles she learned from him into the first tenets of Christian Science.

SEE ALSO James's *The Principles of Psychology* (1890), Mindfulness and Mind-Body Medicine (1993)

WHERE BRAIN FUNCTIONS
ARE LOCALIZED

Paul Broca (1824–80)

FEROCIOUS DEBATES about the nature of the soul, mind, and brain raged throughout the nineteenth century. Were mental functions entirely due to brain activity, or were there certain functions, like reason, that were reserved for divine influence, as French philosopher René Descartes had argued two centuries earlier?

In the nineteenth century, a new generation of scientists turned to the clinical case study and the laboratory experiment to find evidence to support their arguments. One of the most controversial topics was whether mental functions were localized, or restricted to certain areas, in the brain. Franz Gall had developed phrenology, or the study of the surface of the skull, and stated unequivocally that the mind's abilities were entirely attributable to the brain and certain traits were found in specific brain areas. Many sought to discredit Gall's approach, calling

> [Broca's] theory [was] that the ability to speak was localized in the frontal lobe of the brain.

it godless, but by the mid-nineteenth century, evidence was mounting that at least some mental functions were indeed localized in the brain.

Language was one such function, and in 1861 the young French surgeon Paul Broca provided the first concrete evidence with his careful case study of a Monsieur Leborgne, known by the nickname of Tan. Tan, who had lost the ability to speak years earlier, came under Broca's care a few days before he died. Broca realized that this case presented an opportunity to test his theory that the ability to speak was localized in the frontal lobe of the brain; upon autopsy, damage was found in the rear portion of the left frontal lobe. Other cases of language loss and localized brain damage soon were found, and although these findings did not settle the debate conclusively, they provided crucial evidence of the localization of functions. The lack of ability to speak is now known as Broca's aphasia.

After Broca, many other scientists provided evidence of localized function. By the end of the nineteenth century, the study of the brain was firmly in the domain of science, with little need to rely on philosophy or religion.

SEE ALSO Descartes on Mind and Body (1637), The Curious Case of Phineas Gage (1848), Right Brain, Left Brain (1962)

PROSOPAGNOSIA: THE INABILITY TO RECOGNIZE FACES

Antonio Quaglino (1817–94), Giambattista Borelli (1813–91)

THE FRENCH NEUROLOGIST JEAN-MARTIN CHARCOT once had a patient who tried to shake hands with a man who had bumped into him; the other man was himself, reflected in a mirror. This inability to recognize faces, or prosopagnosia, is a relatively rare disorder. It is one of several kinds of visual agnosias, or inability to recognize familiar objects, that is not associated with general intellectual impairment. Nor is it a problem of vision; people suffering from prosopagnosia typically have perfectly good vision. It is a disorder resulting from damage to the brain, usually in both the temporal and parietal lobes. Recently, however, individuals with developmental prosopagnosia, which is present from birth, have been found, indicating a possible genetic basis for face recognition.

Historically the condition was first described, though not named, in the medical literature in 1847. The first full account of a patient, however, came from two Italian ophthalmologists, Antonio Quaglino and Giambattista Borelli, in 1867. They offered a detailed case study of a man who had lost the ability to recognize faces and the exteriors of houses after having a stroke in the right hemisphere of his brain. The term *prosopagnosia* ("face not knowing") was given to the disorder in 1947. More recently, neurologist and author Oliver Sacks gives a fascinating account of prosopagnosia in his book *The Man Who Mistook His Wife for a Hat* (1985).

Curiously, it is not only human faces that are affected by the disorder. There are accounts of farmers who fail to recognize their cows or sheep and bird-watchers who lose the ability to distinguish between species of birds.

People with prosopagnosia have an inability to recognize faces—sometimes even their own face reflected in a mirror. Engraving by Dirk Jurriaan Sluyter, after Cornelis Bisschop, 1857.

Contemporary research using brain imaging techniques such as functional magnetic resonance imaging (fMRI) suggest that face recognition is a special function. Research with primates, including humans, indicates that there are specialized neurons (or brain cells) dedicated to recognizing faces. Apparently, damage to these cells leads to the inability to recognize faces, even our own.

SEE ALSO Seeing the Brain at Work (1924), Mirror Neurons (1992)

SYNESTHESIA: NUMBERS AS COLORS OR TUESDAY IS RED

Gustav Theodor Fechner (1801–87)

SYNESTHESIA IS A CONDITION in which the senses flow into each other, like a house without interior walls. It occurs when a person has an experience in one sense that is accompanied by an involuntary experience in one of the other senses. Reported synesthetic experiences involve sound-color, smell-color, and movement-sound. Some synesthetes, or people affected with synesthesia, experience a day of the week as a person or as a color; the possibilities are numerous. One classic case reported by neuroscientist Richard Cytowic in his book *The Man Who Tasted Shapes* (1993) involved a friend who experienced flavor as shape. At a dinner party, the friend commented about a meal, "There aren't enough points on the chicken! It is too round." The most commonly reported synesthesia is number-color (or letter-color)—for example, the number seven is experienced as red.

The earliest research on synesthesia was conducted by the German philosopher Gustav Fechner. His study, published in 1871, included seventy-three synesthetes who all experienced letters as colors. In 1880, the scientist Francis Galton reported that it appears to run in families, a supposition strongly supported by recent research, including studies by Ramachandran and Hubbard (2001) and Grossenbacher and Lovelace (2001). Interest in synesthesia was strong among early psychologists, such as Alfred Binet and Théodore Flournoy, then waned for a number of years, but it has shown resurgence since the 1980s.

Synesthesia is relatively rare: estimates of its occurrence range from one in two thousand to one in two hundred people, and it is found more frequently among artists, poets, musicians, and novelists. As neuro-scientist V. S. Ramachandran noted about this connection, "One thing these groups of people have in common is a remarkable facility for linking two seemingly unrelated realms in order to highlight a hidden deep similarity."

Synesthetic experiences involve sound-color, smell-color, and movement-sound.

One hypothesis about the cause of synesthesia is that it is due to cross-wiring in the brain. For example, the most common synesthesia, number-color, may reflect such crosswiring between two adjacent areas—one that processes number shapes and one that deals with colors. Many prominent neuroscientists believe that further research on synesthesia will greatly expand our understanding of brain functions and human consciousness.

SEE ALSO Direct Brain Stimulation and Experiential Hallucinations (1941), Neuroplasticity (1948)

NATURE VS. NURTURE

Francis Galton (1822–1911)

IN *HEREDITARY GENIUS* (1869), scientist Sir Francis Galton, a cousin of Charles Darwin, proposed that prominence and genius were largely due to heredity. Galton did not so much discount the influence of the environment as ignore it. French Swiss botanist Adolphe de Candolle disputed Galton's claim and provided statistical evidence of the importance of environmental influences on the development of scientists in his 1873 book *Histoire des sciences et des savants depuis deux siècles*. Galton countered Candolle with his 1874 book *English Men of Science: Their Nature and Nurture*. Galton argued that "nature is all that a man brings with himself into the world, nurture is every influence that affects him after his birth." The phrase was soon turned into *nature vs. nurture*, and the ensuing debate has not been settled yet.

The later development and use of standardized intelligence tests led to fierce arguments about the role of heredity and environment in human intelligence. Studies in the 1920s and 1930s provided evidence that differences between minority and white children in academic achievement were due to cultural, environmental, and linguistic factors rather than innate differences in ethnic intellect. In a series of studies, psychologists found that placing orphaned white children in an atmosphere where they were showered with attention and affection raised their test scores. And perhaps most telling, twin studies demonstrated how raising genetically identical children in different environments can lead to significant differences in both personality and physique.

Still, aided by advances in neuroscience and the study of heredity, many psychologists hold to the overriding importance of nature in numerous domains, from personality to mental disorders to intelligence. It is likely that the debate will never be decided in favor of one view or the other.

Photograph of identical twin infants, c. 1905; twin studies showed how raising genetically identical children (nature) in different environments (nurture) could lead to differences in both personality and physique.

SEE ALSO Tabula Rasa: The Psychology of Experience (1690), Rousseau's Natural Child (1762), Cultural Relativism: Culture, Sex, and Coming of Age (1928), Contact Hypothesis or How to Reduce Racism and Bias (1954)

PSYCHOLOGY BECOMES A SCIENCE

Wilhelm Wundt (1832–1920)

Photogravure of Wilhelm Wundt, 1898.

HAILED AS THE FOUNDER of experimental psychology, Wilhelm Wundt left a multifaceted legacy for modern students of the discipline. His founder status rests in part on a number of important intellectual and institutional firsts. In 1874 he published the first textbook of experimental psychology, *Principles of Physiological Psychology*. Five years later, at Germany's University of Leipzig, he established the first psychological laboratory and trained dozens of new psychologists who flocked to study there and solidify their scientific credentials.

In developing psychology as an experimental discipline, Wundt built on the work of Gustav Fechner, Hermann von Helmholtz, and other psychophysical and physiological researchers by applying systematic, replicable methods to the study of conscious experience. Wundt did this by using often quite elaborate mechanical apparatuses to make standardized presentations of stimuli to subjects who were trained to observe and report their conscious experience of these stimuli. Known as experimental introspection, it was a method that Wundt felt was appropriate for studying the basic properties of the normal adult human mind, such as sensation, perception, and attention.

But here is where Wundt's legacy gets more complex. Wundt felt that higher-order functions, such as thinking, language, personality, social behavior, and customs, could not be studied with these experimental methods but were nonetheless an important, if not central, part of scientific psychology. For this branch of his system he specified comparative and historical methods involving naturalistic observation and logical analysis.

He felt so strongly about this part of psychology that he wrote twelve volumes, entitled *Völkerpsychologie*, on the subject. In this work, he outlined how the study of the products of collective life, including religion, language, and social mores, could provide clues to the higher operations of the mind. This aspect of Wundt's work was largely neglected until historians brought it to light in the 1970s. Thus Wundt not only founded experimental psychology but also defined the limits of its methods.

SEE ALSO Fechner and the Just-Noticeable Difference (JND) (1834), James's *The Principles of Psychology* (1890)

1880

ANNA O.: CONVERTING PSYCHOLOGICAL DISTRESS INTO PHYSICAL ILLNESS

Josef Breuer (1842–1925), Sigmund Freud (1856–1939)

THE IDEA THAT HUMAN BEINGS convert their psychological distress into physical symptoms is the basis of what is now called somatoform disorder. It has a long and rich history linked to the beginning of psychoanalysis. Patients suffering from hysteria in the nineteenth century often displayed unusual physical symptoms, many of which were found to be neurologically impossible—for example, in the condition known as glove anesthesia, the patient reports no sensation below the wrist but upon examination the doctor can find no neurological cause.

> According to Freud . . . conversion occurs when a mental image, impulse, or desire is incompatible with [the] ego.

Physician Josef Breuer discussed the case of "Anna O." with neurologist Sigmund Freud early in their professional relationship. In 1880, Breuer had treated the young woman, whose real name was Bertha Pappenheim, for a variety of symptoms that emerged as she cared for her dying father.

Freud and Breuer's work on the case of Anna O. is part of the origin of the notion of "conversion." According to Freud, the inclination toward conversion was characteristic of hysterical patients. The conversion occurs when a mental image, impulse, or desire is incompatible with the part of our psychic apparatus that Freud termed the ego. In order to deal with the stress, the emotion associated with the unacceptable image is dismissed from consciousness by means of repression. The energy, however, remains and is converted into a sensory-motor disturbance that symbolizes and physically expresses the unacceptable content. This solves, at least temporarily, the original psychological conflict.

The transformation does not happen by chance. Freud suggested that the chosen bodily function is always one that has been invested with special significance in some special moment of life. In this sense, the body part or function held a particular symbolic meaning.

For many years, conversion disorder was a common diagnosis. As the field of psychosomatic medicine developed in the 1930s, it played an important theoretical role, exemplified in the belief that stress and worry could cause a peptic ulcer, for example. Curiously, the number of diagnosed cases of conversion disorder greatly diminished in the last third of the twentieth century.

SEE ALSO Psychoanalysis: The Talking Cure (1899), The Discovery of Stress (1950)

MULTIPLE PERSONALITY DISORDER

Pierre Janet (1859–1947)

A double-exposure photograph from c. 1885 shows English actor and writer Richard Mansfield in character as both protagonists in the stage play *Dr. Jekyll and Mr. Hyde*. The story is probably the most vivid and well-known portrayal of the split personality.

WHILE COLLECTING MATERIAL for his doctoral dissertation in 1885, the young philosophy student and teacher Pierre Janet first described the case of Léonie, a woman with the unusual ability to be hypnotized from a distance. In addition, when she was under hypnosis, it became evident that Léonie had three distinct selves. Further experiments with her and other subjects—all of whom had more than one personality—were detailed in Janet's book *Psychological Automatism* (1889). The book caused a sensation in the medical and psychological worlds. Janet coined the term *dissociation* to indicate the condition of experiencing a split in a person's sense of self. When Janet's work received wider recognition, others began reporting cases of split or multiple personalities as well.

In 1957, the movie *The Three Faces of Eve* fictionalized the case of an American woman with three personalities: Eve White, Eve Black, and Jane, each of them with seemingly independent lives. The movie brought the concept of multiple personalities back into popular culture, but in the 1980s and 1990s the disorder, now renamed dissociative identity disorder, or DID, seemed to be everywhere, with several well-known individuals revealing that they had multiple personalities.

The diagnostic criteria for DID include at least two more or less complete systems of identity, with the person switching from one to the other, usually for short periods of time. The host personality is usually the best defined, while the alter identities may vary wildly from the host. The number of alter identities varies, ranging from two to as many as fifteen. Currently, alter identities are not conceptualized as completely separate personalities; rather they are displays of conflicts, feelings, and memories, acted out in a very stylized manner. Still, just as with Léonie, these cases fascinate us with their demonstrations of the complexity of personhood.

SEE ALSO Psychoanalysis: The Talking Cure (1899), Projective Tests: The Rorschach Inkblots (1921)

1886

PSYCHOPATHIA SEXUALIS

Richard von Krafft-Ebing (1840–1902)

THE TERMS *SADISM*, indicating the enjoyment of sexual violence, and *masochism*, or the enjoyment of having violence inflicted on oneself for pleasure, were popularized by German psychiatrist Richard von Krafft-Ebing. He was writing at a time when there was concern that the great achievements of German *Kultur* were being lost to degeneration, which he took to mean the inheritable consequences of immoral behavior. Nor was he alone, as many of his fellow psychiatrists and physicians were warning of the same evil. In this they were anticipating the eugenics of the early twentieth century.

Most worrisome, Krafft-Ebing believed, were the sexual pathologies that seemed to be occurring with increasing frequency. He set himself to the task of cataloging and classifying these pathologies, and he illustrated them with extremely vivid examples so that they would serve as a warning and deterrent to all who read them. It may well have been that they had the opposite effect.

In more than two hundred case studies, Krafft-Ebing explained the origins and course of sexual pathologies. He divided the abnormalities into broad categories, which included excessive desire, inadequate sexual desire, and misdirected sexual desire; it was in this latter grouping that he placed homosexuality and bisexuality. What was unique about his writing on homosexuality was the emphasis on its biological origins.

After the first edition of *Psychopathia Sexualis* was published in 1886, Krafft-Ebing began receiving letters from individuals who were not patients in an asylum; rather, they wrote because they had learned from the book that they were not the only sadists or masochists. In this way, one could argue that Krafft-Ebing's classification of sexual pathologies helped create modern sexual identities. His case histories made such behaviors appear to be part of the natural world rather than mere vices.

This illustration by Aubrey Beardsley from 1895—the frontispiece to the comical novel *A Full and True Account of the Wonderful Mission of Earl Lavender* by John Davidson—depicts a dominatrix-type female figure whipping a kneeling man.

SEE ALSO Masters and Johnson's *Human Sexual Response* (1966), Diamond's *Sexual Fluidity* (2008)

JAMES'S *THE PRINCIPLES OF PSYCHOLOGY*

William James (1842–1910)

ARTISTIC BY TEMPERAMENT, William James bowed to his father's wishes and was educated as a physician. He never practiced, however, and after a period of existential struggle he accepted an appointment as a lecturer at Harvard. There he pioneered the new field of psychology in America and wrote what proved to be the most influential text of his era, *The Principles of Psychology*. It took him twelve years to write, and after it was published in 1890 he wrote a friend, "Psychology is a damnable subject."

[James] said consciousness is like a stream, dynamic and ever changing.

In *Principles*, James described psychology as the science of mental life. He wrote that the point of scientific psychology was to help us understand that consciousness and our minds evolved to help us adapt and survive in the world. Thus what consciousness does is more important than what it is or what it contains.

How might the mind best be studied? In Germany, the first laboratory psychologists were using refined mechanical instruments such as the Hipp chronoscope to measure mental reactions. James rejected this approach, as he believed that one could never understand the complexity of human mental life by adding up its contents or by measuring the speed of reactions. James offered an alternative view of consciousness. In a beautiful and enduring metaphor, he said consciousness is like a stream, dynamic and ever changing. A person, he wrote, could never step into the same river twice. Thus no instrument could ever capture this experience.

James also wrote about habit, calling it the "flywheel of life." He proposed a theory of emotions, that feelings follow behavior, which now is known as the James-Lange theory of emotions. (Carl Lange was a Danish physician who made the same suggestion independently but at about the same time.) James also argued for a pragmatic, pluralistic view of truth; those things are true, he argued, that help us in life.

James and his book have been the greatest influence on the development of American psychology to date. To indicate his breadth, it is worth noting his obituary headline in the *New York Times*: "William James Dies; Great Psychologist, brother of novelist, and foremost American philosopher was 68 years old. Long Harvard professor, virtual founder of modern American psychology, and exponent of pragmatism, dabbled in spooks."

SEE ALSO Mind-Cure (1859), Psychology Becomes a Science (1874)

WESTERN CULTURAL BIAS: THE TORRES STRAITS EXPEDITION

William H. R. Rivers (1864–1922)

NEAR THE END OF THE NINETEENTH CENTURY, a small group of men interested in anthropological questions organized a seven-month expedition to the Torres Strait Islands, a group of small islands located in the strait between Australia and New Guinea. The team, led by British anthropologist Alfred Cort Haddon, recruited a young physician and psychologist at Cambridge University, William H. R. Rivers, to go with them.

Rivers, whose specialty was vision, was in charge of the psychological investigations of the islanders. To assist him, he recruited two young psychologists, C. S. Myers, who later coined the phrase *shell shock*, and William McDougall. He and his colleagues conducted an elaborate psychological assessment of vision and other sensory and motor abilities, using laboratory equipment adapted for the purpose. More than twenty psychological or psychophysiological phenomena were studied, including olfactory discrimination, vision, pitch threshold, and color perception.

A primary rationale for the research was that the Torres Strait's inhabitants had not had much exposure to the norms and mores of Western industrialized countries. Thus they were truly naive about the hypotheses of the research. As Rivers wrote, "The people are sufficiently civilized to enable us to make all our observations, and yet they were sufficiently near their primitive condition to be thoroughly interesting." Rivers and his team found, however, that they could not use introspection as one of their methods, since the concept was totally foreign to the islanders.

The psychologists discovered that, contrary to the myth of heightened sensory powers associated with the "noble savage," most of the sensory abilities tested were in ranges similar to those of Europeans. The psychological research of the expedition also demonstrated that psychology had the methods and the tools to test and clarify knowledge that previously had been based on a priori assumptions or traditions of European superiority. By offering empirical evidence that refuted older claims of racial superiority, the expedition's results opened the door to explanations based on differing environmental experiences. This proved to be important in the race and intelligence debates that emerged in the 1920s and 1930s in American psychology.

> The psychologists discovered that . . . most of the sensory abilities tested were in ranges similar to those of Europeans.

SEE ALSO Culture Determines What Counts as Mental Illness (1904)

PSYCHOANALYSIS: THE TALKING CURE

Sigmund Freud (1856–1939)

TRAINED IN VIENNA as a neurologist by the leading medical scientists of his day, Sigmund Freud used reason to show that humans often are motivated by forces of unreason, including sex, anger, and fear. His ideas have

Sigmund Freud poses for a portrait with fellow psychoanalysts at the Sixth International Psychoanalytic Congress in the Hague, September 1920: first row, seated—Freud (center), Ernest Jones (second from left), Sándor Ferenczi (second from right); Karl Abraham stands in the second row (third from left).

been explored in literature, drama, painting, and architecture in addition to the clinical fields of psychiatry, psychology, social work, and counseling.

Freud was an excellent student with a voracious intellectual curiosity who chose medicine as his life's work. His education sensitized him to the importance of motivation and the dynamic character of human behavior. His desire to be a great scientist led to six years in a laboratory doing careful studies of the nervous systems of fish and other creatures. After he fell in love with Martha Bernays, he became a clinician in order to have an income suitable for supporting a family.

A fellowship in Paris with the noted neurologist Jean-Martin Charcot led to the clinical insight that trauma plays a role in hysteria by causing ideas to become dissociated from rational thought. Upon his return to Vienna, he learned about the talking cure that his mentor, Josef Breuer, had applied in the case of Anna O. in 1880. All of this was used by Freud to formulate the first principles of psychoanalysis. He developed the techniques of dream analysis and free association to gain access to his patients' unconscious. He also first described the clinical phenomena of repression, transference, and countertransference, which became the bedrock of psychoanalytic practice.

Until his death, Freud continued to refine his theory, as he constantly learned from the application of his ideas in an active clinical practice. Freud theorized about children's development, the origin of neuroses, the role of instinctual behavior, and the emergence and use of psychological defense mechanisms. He wrote about the role of religion, which he called an illusion, and articulated why civilization created psychological conflicts. His theoretical and clinical work was the primary contributor to the creation of psychological subjectivity during the twentieth century.

SEE ALSO Anna O.: Converting Psychological Distress into Physical Illness (1880), *The Interpretation of Dreams* Inaugurates the Century of Psychology (1900), Jungian Psychology: Collective Unconscious and Psychological Growth (1913), Defense Mechanisms (1936)

1900

THE INTERPRETATION OF DREAMS
INAUGURATES THE CENTURY
OF PSYCHOLOGY

Sigmund Freud (1856–1939)

THE FOUNDATIONAL PRINCIPLES for psychoanalysis were developed by Sigmund Freud from 1886 to 1900. At the end of this period, he published his most important book, *The Interpretation of Dreams*. The book proposed an entirely psychological, rather than neurological, model of the mind. Although Freud constantly revised most of his theories, most of this book's major ideas were articulated in terms that he did not later modify or revise.

The immediate origin of the book's topic was the death of his father, Jakob, which occurred in 1896. The event caused deep turmoil in Freud's life and left him depressed. After several months, he decided to act as if he were a patient and, using dreams and free association, to analyze himself. It was through this self-analysis that Freud found in dreams the "royal road to the unconscious." His analysis of dreams led him to suggest that dreams have two levels of meaning: the manifest content, which is superficial and does not contain the real psychological meaning of the dream, and the latent content, which is the real meaning dressed in symbolic form.

> It was through . . . self-analysis that Freud found in dreams the "royal road to the unconscious."

Dreams, Freud suggested, are wish fulfillments whose latent meaning is intended to disguise their socially unacceptable nature. In this way dreams are like symptoms of hysteria, in that both represent ideas or wishes that are too dangerous to be expressed in everyday life. Here Freud had a great insight: he had previously supposed that his patients' reports of childhood sexual experiences represented actual events. Now he saw that these experiences had probably not happened; rather, his patients' memories of them were sexual wishes expressed in symbolic form.

When Freud began to use free association to analyze his own dreams after his father's death, he was shocked to discover many of the same types of wishes in his own dream life. Of greatest importance was his discovery through self-analysis of the existence of the Oedipus complex, a principle that proved critically important for his later work on the development of personality.

SEE ALSO Psychoanalysis: The Talking Cure (1899), Jungian Psychology: Collective Unconscious and Psychological Growth (1913), Defense Mechanisms (1936)

FORENSIC PSYCHOLOGY

William Stern (1871–1938)

This early twentieth-century photograph depicts a fictional scene of a woman being sworn in before giving her testimony in a courtroom.

STANDARDS FOR WHO IS QUALIFIED to offer testimony in a court of law evolved along with the codification of law. For most of recorded history, women and children were forbidden to testify, as it was believed that they could not be credible. Many other classes of individuals—such as slaves, criminals, and the poor—have also been excluded at various times. By the beginning of the twentieth century, however, the possibility of improving testimony was suggested by psychologists.

German psychologist William Stern was the first to do applied research on the psychology of testimony. Previously, in late-1870s Germany, the first laboratories of experimental psychology were established; by the 1890s Germans had developed a full-fledged study of applied psychology, too. In 1902, as Stern initiated his research program on legal psychology, the first courses were being offered on law and psychology at various universities. For example, Max Wertheimer, best known as the founder of Gestalt psychology, completed his dissertation on determining the truthfulness of testimony in 1904. In the United States, the first application of psychology to the study of testimony was made by German émigré psychologist Hugo Münsterberg in 1908.

An enduring problem in the psychology of testimony has been the disjuncture between laboratory studies, where many variables can be controlled, and the complexity and messiness of actual trials. Nevertheless, by the 1980s in the United States, a robust body of research findings began to accumulate. Eyewitness testimony has become a particularly problematic arena: on the one hand, psychologists have developed expertise in how to improve the questioning of witnesses as well as methods to elicit reliable testimony. On the other hand, psychologists have also shown that memory is easily manipulated and thus unreliable, as in the case of false memory syndrome.

SEE ALSO Psychology Becomes a Science (1874), The Lie Detector and the Golden Lasso of Truth (1913), Remembering and Forgetting (1932)

CLASSICAL CONDITIONING: PAVLOV'S BELL

Ivan Pavlov (1849–1936)

RUSSIAN PHYSIOLOGIST IVAN PAVLOV insisted that the scientific study of the nervous system and its expressions must be objective, mechanistic, and materialistic in orientation. Pavlov was born and reared in central Russia, the son of a village priest. Initially, it seemed as though Pavlov would follow in his father's footsteps, but a growing personal interest in science led him to the University of Saint Petersburg, where he earned a degree in physiology.

By 1890, Pavlov was the director of the department of physiology at the university's Institute of Experimental Medicine. Pavlov's specialty was the study of digestion, for which he was awarded the Nobel Prize in physiology or medicine in 1904. Dogs were Pavlov's subject of choice for

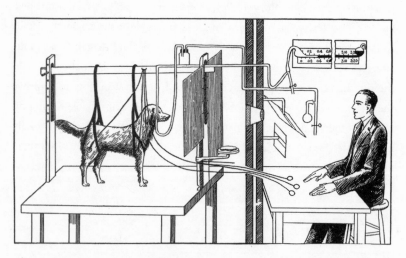

A diagram illustrating classical conditioning on a dog, from a 1941 edition of Ivan Pavlov's *Lectures on Conditioned Reflexes* (1928).

his experiments. When his work on digestion in the stomach came to an end, Pavlov began to study salivation as a necessary part of the digestive processes. In 1903, one of the dog handlers in Pavlov's laboratory observed that the dogs began salivation even before they were fed. When this came to Pavlov's attention, he experimentally investigated what he called the "psychic processes" involved in the phenomenon.

Pavlov explored how external stimuli could be manipulated to control behavior. His most famous example came to be called classical conditioning in English. It was a convincing demonstration that when a ringing bell is presented in association with the offering of food, dogs will become conditioned, or learn, to salivate even without food being offered. Pavlov claimed that such conditioning was a matter of processes in the nervous system itself and not a matter of the mind. Thus learning in the dog, and by extension in humans and other animals, was a matter of forming elementary associations that then led to the formation of chains of associations. For many years, Pavlov and his team explored the implications of his model of learning, including how it might explain mental disorders.

SEE ALSO Experimental Neurosis: How Animals Can Be Made Crazy (1912)

CULTURE DETERMINES WHAT COUNTS AS MENTAL ILLNESS

Emil Kraepelin (1856–1926), Arthur Kleinman (b. 1941)

ARE PSYCHIATRIC DISORDERS best understood within a particular cultural context? That is, are they culture-bound? A growing body of evidence indicates that we cannot assume that human beings experience mental and emotional distress in the same ways or that treatment of such distress is easily exportable from one culture to another. While cultural differences in mentality have been noted for centuries, it was psychiatrist German Emil Kraepelin who wrote about the necessity of taking cultural considerations into account in 1904:

> The characteristics of a people should find expression in the frequency as well as in the shaping of the manifestations of mental illness . . . so that comparative psychiatry shall make it possible to gain valuable insights into the psyche of nations and shall in turn also be able to contribute to the understanding of pathological psychic processes.

It was initially the fieldwork of medical anthropologists that raised questions about the role of culture in health and disease, including mental health. American psychiatrist Arthur Kleinman's *Patients and Healers in the Context of Culture: An Exploration of the Borderland between Anthropology, Medicine, and Psychiatry* (1980) helped set off the contemporary debate on culture-bound syndromes. And American psychologist Anthony Marsella has written extensively about culture and depression, pointing out that in many cultures, depression is often expressed through the body, with such symptoms as back pain or stomach distress.

Some behaviors are culturally prescribed ways of describing distress.

In recent years, there has finally been recognition by American psychiatrists that some behaviors are culturally prescribed ways of describing distress that may or may not have psychopathological significance. Two culture-bound syndromes will serve as examples:

* **KORO** (East and Southeast Asia, Africa): an episode of sudden and intense anxiety in which it is believed that one's penis (or in the rare female cases, the vulva or nipples) will shrink or recede into the body and possibly cause death.

* **ANOREXIA NERVOSA** (North America, Western Europe): severe restriction of food intake, associated with morbid fear of obesity.

These syndromes indicate the important role that cultural beliefs and mores play in determining mental health and illness.

SEE ALSO Western Cultural Bias: The Torres Straits Expedition (1898)

BINET AND SIMON: THE FIRST INTELLIGENCE TEST

Alfred Binet (1857–1911), Théodore Simon (1872–1961)

BY THE EARLY TWENTIETH CENTURY, France had fallen behind its archrival Germany in industrial production. To catch up, pressure was exerted on schools to do a better job educating French children. The teachers complained, however, that classes were too large and that too many "subnormal" children were mixed in with those of "normal" ability.

To help them solve this problem, the French government turned to Alfred Binet, a psychologist known for his work with children. Binet's first attempt to develop tests failed. He was then joined by Théodore Simon, a young physician who worked at a large institution for the mentally impaired. Binet and Simon could now compare the results of their tests with children of both average and below-average ability.

> Binet and Simon developed a set of thirty tasks of increasing levels of difficulty.

Binet had an important insight: although both groups of children were able to pass the same kinds of tests, the normal children did so at a younger age than the subnormal children. With this insight, Binet and Simon developed a set of thirty tasks of increasing levels of difficulty, starting with very simple tasks, such as shaking hands with the tester, up to very complex tasks that even the oldest children had difficulty with, such as defining abstract words. Children would then progress through the tests, stopping at the point where they could no longer pass. Their achievement would be noted and compared to the age corresponding to that level. This was referred to as the child's "mental level." Any child who fell two years or more behind his or her age peers in performance was identified as subnormal and could be placed in a class appropriate to his or her mental level.

The Binet-Simon test, first published in 1905, underwent revisions in 1908 and 1911, and it was adapted for use in America in 1916. Binet continued to believe that intelligence was not fixed and that a test such as his should not be used to predict future performance: it was only a snapshot in time.

The American revision was called the Stanford-Binet Intelligence Scale; it yielded a measure of intelligence that could be expressed as a number, the intelligence quotient (IQ), a term borrowed from German psychologist William Stern (1871–1938). The Stanford-Binet test assumes an innate, unchangeable, individual intellectual ability, though research continues to make these assumptions doubtful.

SEE ALSO Projective Tests: The Rorschach Inkblots (1921), Thematic Apperception Test: Our Stories and Our Personality (1935)

1908

BLEULER INITIATES THE MODERN STUDY OF THE SCHIZOPHRENIAS

Paul Eugen Bleuler (1857–1939)

WHAT WE NOW REFER TO AS SCHIZOPHRENIA has almost certainly existed throughout human history, but it was not until 1908 that it was given its current label by psychiatrist Eugen Bleuler. At the time, Bleuler was the director of the leading psychiatric hospital in Europe, the Burghölzli, in Switzerland. He became its director in 1898, and during his tenure many of the leading figures in psychiatry worked with him, including Carl Jung and Hermann Rorschach. Bleuler disagreed with the existing term for the condition, *dementia praecox*, because his clinical experience showed him that patients did not typically become demented, nor was the onset always in youth (the meaning of the word *praecox*).

The schizophrenias are characterized by delusions, hallucinations, and disordered thought. The subtypes of the disorder are catatonic, disorganized, paranoid, and undifferentiated. Each subtype has its own characteristic patterns. The paranoid type, for example, may have delusions of persecution or grandeur, as one patient explained in the following passage from Bleuler's *Dementia Praecox, oder Gruppe der Schizophrenien* (*Dementia Praecox, or Group of Schizophrenias*) (1911): "Inside it is as if I were Christ or the Apostles. Twenty-six Apostles are on the Mount of Olives in my arms."

It is not uncommon for multiple patients in the same hospital to have identical delusions, as in the famous case of the "three Christs of Ypsilianti"; in a hospital in the Washington, DC, area, two patients, similar in age, both believed they were the legitimate sons of John F. Kennedy. It also is common for those suffering from one of the schizophrenias to invent neologisms, or to coin new meaningless words and phrases: for example, one person might spit "cage-weather juice," while others have been "botanized" or "blued-off."

Despite more than a hundred years of research, there is no known cause for schizophrenia; it is likely that there are multiple causes. The study of identical twins indicates a strong genetic component. A 2012 report indicated that at least five disorders share a common genetic link: schizophrenia, bipolar disorder, autism, major depression, and attention deficit hyperactivity disorder.

> Despite more than a hundred years of research, there is no known cause for schizophrenia.

SEE ALSO Bipolar Disorder and Creativity (1851)

CAN APES LEARN HUMAN LANGUAGE?

Lightner Witmer (1867–1956), William H. Furness III (1867–1920)

PHILADELPHIA IN 1909 WITNESSED a remarkable demonstration by Peter, a sophisticated chimpanzee. Peter appeared on stage and skated, rode a bicycle, ate with a fork, and smoked a cigarette. Peter was "born a monkey and made himself a man," according to publicity for the show. Two men observed the show very carefully—psychologist Lightner Witmer and famed explorer William H. Furness III. Witmer, who had recently established a psychology clinic to help children with problems that included speech and language, speculated whether an ape as intelligent as Peter could be taught to talk. Peter got no further than *mama*, but Furness was able to teach a companion orangutan two words: *papa* and *cup*.

There had long been fascination among comparative psychologists and other natural scientists about the capacity of apes to learn human speech and whether apes had a language of their own. On the latter question, explorer and scientist Richard Garner documented ape vocalizations in the wild that appeared to be a form of communication. Garner's claims were supported by psychologist Robert Yerkes, who in the 1920s identified at least thirty-two word-like sounds that two chimps used.

In the 1930s, two psychologists, Luella and Winthrop Kellogg, raised a young female chimp named Gua in their home alongside their infant son. Gua did not learn to talk but clearly understood many words. Twenty years later, a baby chimp, Viki, was brought to live with psychologists Keith and Catherine Hayes. Viki lived to be seven and learned a few words: *mama*, *papa*, and *cup*. Again, Viki understood quite a few words and also succeeded in teaching Cathy several chimp vocalizations. In the 1960s, Washoe, a chimpanzee, learned to correctly use more than thirty signs and understood many others. Since then, a variety of methods have been used to try to teach apes to communicate using some kind of symbolic language. The jury is still out.

Two baboons sitting on a log face each other in what seems to be a pause during a deep conversation.

SEE ALSO Darwin's *On the Origin of Species* (1859), Theory of Mind (1978)

1912

GESTALT PSYCHOLOGY: THE WHOLE IS GREATER THAN THE SUM OF ITS PARTS

Max Wertheimer (1880–1943), Kurt Koffka (1886–1941), Wolfgang Köhler (1887–1967)

BEGINNING AROUND 1910, a group of young psychologists—Max Wertheimer, Kurt Koffka, and Wolfgang Köhler—began to develop the Gestalt theory in psychology during an era in which personal and national wholeness became an important part of the fabric of German life. They called their approach Gestalt theory, though it is more often referred to as Gestalt psychology. (The term *Gestalt* has no exact equivalent in English, but roughly corresponds to "form" or "configuration.")

Wertheimer published his experimental results on apparent movement, the so-called phi phenomenon, in 1912. The perceived motion, he argued, was a Gestalt and not reducible to individual elements; thus it was not explicable in terms of associations. The insistence on studying the relationship between the part and the whole in terms of perception and cognition led the Gestalt psychologists away from the analysis of the constituents, or individual elements, of mental structures and psychic processes.

The Gestalt psychologists developed an approach that articulated the psychological richness of life. Wertheimer, his peers, and their students brought their relational research to studies of perception (e.g., figure-ground relationships), language, symbolic thought, and insight in ways that yielded new understandings. They conducted their work in the service of helping to solve philosophical problems, especially questions of epistemology and cognition.

Perceptual organization remains the best-known example of Gestalt theory. The most general principle is the law of Prägnanz, which states that there is a tendency toward the organization of any whole or Gestalt into as good or as simple a structure as conditions permit. Specific examples of the law of Prägnanz include the laws of proximity, similarity, continuation, and closure. Although the Gestalt theorists all left Germany under duress during the Nazi era and were never able to gain equivalent positions in the United States, their influence in our current era remains in social and cognitive psychology.

Max Wertheimer, a founder of Gestalt psychology, with a tachistoscope, a key psychological laboratory instrument of the period, used to present visual stimuli for controlled durations.

SEE ALSO Conformity and Independence (1951), Cognitive Dissonance: How Humans Maintain Psychological Consistency (1957)

1912

EXPERIMENTAL NEUROSIS: HOW ANIMALS CAN BE MADE CRAZY

Mariya Yerofeyeva (1867–1925),
Nataliya Shenger-Krestovnikova (1875–1947)

IVAN PAVLOV'S LABORATORY OF PHYSIOLOGY at the Institute of Experimental Medicine in Saint Petersburg, Russia, was a busy place in the early twentieth century. The laboratory was a massive enterprise, with hundreds of employees working in a factory-like setting. Pavlov demonstrated that animals can be conditioned to salivate in response to a stimulus other than food.

After the classical conditioning paradigm was developed, Pavlov assigned research scientists to explore its possible variations. Two women scientists were assigned the task of investigating disruptions in the conditioned response. In this set of experiments, dogs were conditioned to respond (salivate) to a circle that had been paired with food, but to not respond when an ellipse was presented (the ellipse was not paired with food). Once conditioning was established, then the ellipse was altered to look more and more like a circle in successive conditioning trials. At first, the dogs could discriminate between the two stimuli and would only salivate when the circle was presented. As the ellipse was altered and discrimination became more and more difficult, the dogs became visibly upset, barked repeatedly, and acted aggressively. Pavlov believed that these results had implications for human mental disorders.

Two Americans, W. H. Gantt of Johns Hopkins University and H. S. Liddell of Cornell University, took up the study of what was by then called experimental neurosis. The same response was found in a number of species, including goats, sheep, pigs, rabbits, and cats. Both Gantt and Liddell wrote extensively about the implications of the results for human mental disorders. The field of psychosomatic medicine was then just beginning, and many thought it possible to connect psychoanalytic theory and experimental neurosis research to explain psychosomatic disorders. Out of this pioneering research, the research field known as experimental psychopathology emerged. One of its major findings was the theory of learned helplessness.

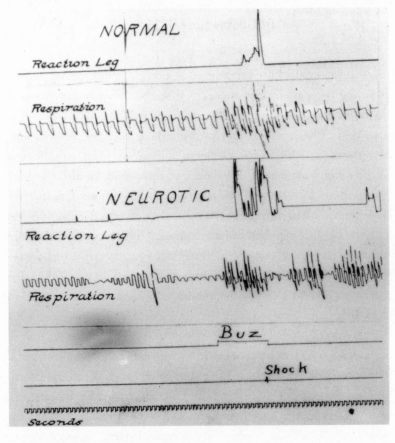

H. S. Liddell induced experimental neurosis in a variety of species. Here, a graph of "normal" and "neurotic" sheep responses to a shock experiment.

SEE ALSO Classical Conditioning: Pavlov's Bell (1903)

1913

JUNGIAN PSYCHOLOGY: COLLECTIVE UNCONSCIOUS AND PSYCHOLOGICAL GROWTH

Carl Gustav Jung (1875–1961)

CARL JUNG REPORTED THAT, even as a child, he experienced himself as having two personalities, one current and one from an earlier era. A bright child and good student, Jung eventually decided on psychiatry as a career. In 1900, after earning his medical degree in Switzerland, Jung began working with Eugen Bleuler at the leading psychiatric hospital in the world, Switzerland's Burghölzli. In this period, he discovered the early writings of Freud and was invited to Vienna to meet him in 1907. They formed a friendship and even traveled together to the United States in 1909. On that trip they had an unpleasant disagreement when Freud refused to divulge a dream he had the night before, contrary to their agreement to share and analyze each other's dreams every morning. The disagreement eventually led to the unraveling of their relationship, and in 1913, Jung broke away and spent the remainder of his life developing what he called depth psychology.

Jung proposed both a personal unconscious and a collective unconscious. The latter is the repository of the psychological experience of the human race and the source of our most powerful and important ideas and feelings. Material from the collective unconscious takes the form of archetypes, the basic truths of the human experience in symbolic form. These archetypes create our psychological infrastructure. For example, the mother archetype is represented by, among others, Mother Nature and the Virgin Mary. The structures of personality are also archetypes: the ego, the persona, the shadow, and so on.

The goal of our life is psychological growth, which Jung called individuation. We have an innate drive to fully realize our potential as a person; thus this is a dynamic process that unfolds over a lifetime. Naturally, there are obstacles to growth that we must face and overcome; materials we may use to aid our growth include a therapist, our dreams, and our relationships.

A photograph of Carl Gustav Jung standing in front of the Burghölzli psychiatric hospital in Zurich, Switzerland, c. 1909.

SEE ALSO Psychoanalysis: The Talking Cure (1899), Projective Tests: The Rorschach Inkblots (1921), Thematic Apperception Test: Our Stories and Our Personality (1935)

THE LIE DETECTOR AND THE GOLDEN LASSO OF TRUTH

William Moulton Marston (1893–1947)

DECEPTION IS COMMONPLACE between people and by businesses. In the late nineteenth and early twentieth centuries, Western industrialized nations increasingly became consumer societies, and the problem of how to accurately detect deception became an important question. The new sciences of humanity—psychology, sociology, criminology, anthropology— were consulted for insights into how to determine the truth and its companion, the lie.

In 1895, Italian criminologist Cesare Lombroso offered a very crude and unreliable device for use by the police. In 1913, Harvard undergraduate William Marston invented a device that used changes in systolic blood pressure to indicate the likelihood of deception. In 1914, Italian psychologist Vittorio Benussi invented the pneumograph, which used changes in breathing to detect lying.

Marston went on to earn a law degree and a doctorate in psychology after World War I. As the first professor of the psychology of law in the United States, Marston pursued research on emotionality and deception at American University in Washington, D.C. He billed himself as the father of the lie detector, but in 1921, John Larson of the University of California combined Marston's use of changes in systolic blood pressure with his own idea of measuring changes in the galvanic skin response to create a more reliable instrument. One of Larson's protégés later invented a portable lie detector.

The Larson lie detector was the first to be used widely in police work, although it was not universally trusted. The common strategy used by law enforcement for many years was the "third degree," the brutal face-to-face confrontation of a suspect in the hopes of a breakdown and confession, but courts became unsympathetic to this approach. In contrast, the lie detector offered hope of a scientific counterweight to deception. In the United States, each state has its own laws about the admissibility of polygraph evidence, while in federal courts it is up to the judge whether it is admissible.

> Marston invented a device that used changes in systolic blood pressure to indicate the likelihood of deception.

There is a curious footnote to the lie detector. William Marston later created the comic book character Wonder Woman, whose golden lasso of truth was the equivalent of a lie detector.

SEE ALSO Forensic Psychology (1902)

VARIABILITY HYPOTHESIS: GENDER AND GENIUS

Leta Stetter Hollingworth (1886–1939)

A COMMONLY HELD BELIEF originating early in the nineteenth century, the variability hypothesis states that men exhibit greater variability than women across both mental and physical traits. For example, it was commonly believed throughout the nineteenth and early twentieth centuries that men varied more than women in their intellectual ability, thus occupying more of both the upper and lower ends of the intelligence spectrum. Since women were less variable, they were also doomed to mediocrity; only men could attain genius.

Charles Darwin's theory of evolution by natural selection buttressed this conviction in male superiority. Since evolutionary progress was dependent on a healthy pool of genetic variability, the greater variability of the males of the species was seen as desirable. Although empirically unsupported, this belief was used by many social scientists to justify educational and occupational restrictions for women.

The variability hypothesis was not seriously challenged until the work of psychologist Leta Stetter Hollingworth, who in 1914 published an extensive review of the literature that debunked the notion of greater variability in males. Hollingworth carried out a large-scale study of one thousand male and one thousand female infants at the New York Infirmary for Women and Children. She found that while males were slightly larger physically than females, anatomical variability actually favored the females. She also conducted a systematic review of the literature and found no evidence to support the hypothesis for female intellectual inferiority.

Finally, she reasoned that even if the scores of males were more variable than those of females on tests of mental traits, this alone would not prove that greater variability was innate, since men and women experienced entirely different environments and social expectations. Although Hollingworth's research led to a rejection of the variability hypothesis, the idea occasionally receives attention from research psychologists to this day.

A group of infants with their parents at a settlement house in Lower Manhattan, New York City, c. 1914. In a study of one thousand infants at this time in New York, Leta Stetter Hollingworth found that the males were usually slightly larger physically than females, but that anatomical variability actually favored the females.

SEE ALSO Darwin's *On the Origin of Species* (1859), Sex Roles (1944)

TRANSFORMING WESTERN PSYCHOLOGY IN INDIA

Girindrasekhar Bose (1887–1953), Durganand Sinha (1922–98)

AS EARLY AS THE MID-NINETEENTH CENTURY in India, there was interest in psychology as understood in the European sense. The prominent Indian scientist Mahendra Lal Sircar argued that psychology was important in understanding both the objective and subjective aspects of human mentality.

Psychology as an academic discipline was institutionalized in India early in the twentieth century, as indicated by the establishment of the country's first psychological laboratory in 1915 at Calcutta University. Within twenty years, psychology was taught in at least one hundred Indian academic institutions. According to Indian scholars, much of the psychological science in India was derivative of Western psychology in the period between the World Wars and for a period after its independence from Great Britain in 1947. On the other hand, psychoanalysis in India developed in a way that expressed the richness of Indian cultural life.

The pioneer of psychoanalysis in India, Girindrasekhar Bose, transformed psychoanalysis to reflect the reality of Hindu family life and customs, with its emphasis on the mother-son relationship. Bose argued that the most important relationship for psychological development was that of mother and son rather than father and son, as in Freudian theory. Bose proposed that a child wishes to be both male and female; there is not the strong identification with the opposite-sex parent that is the basis for Freud's Oedipus complex. It is, in Bose's view, the contending and opposite wishes that create the need for repression in childhood, the resolution of which holds the promise of healthy personality development. In this way, Indian psychoanalysis became a model for efforts since the 1970s to make Indian psychology reflective of Indian life and relationships.

After World War II, Durganand Sinha did for academic psychology what Bose had done for psychoanalysis. Sinha argued that Indian identity is primarily relational, and, in order to be effective, psychology must originate from this basic, taken-for-granted truth of Indian life.

A watercolor painting of an Indian mother and her infant son. Girindrasekhar Bose argued that the most important relationship for psychological development was that of mother and son rather than father and son, as in Freudian theory.

SEE ALSO Bhagavad Gita (c. 200 BCE), Nurturant-Task Model of Leadership (1980)

ARMY INTELLIGENCE TESTS AND SCIENTIFIC RACISM

Robert Yerkes (1876–1956)

Beginning in the nineteenth century, new theories were deployed to argue that some races were more evolved than others. In the early twentieth century, a new tool—the intelligence test—emerged, and though sorting races was not its creator's intent, it soon was used to "prove" that some groups were intellectually superior. This was also the time when the word *race* became more directly associated with skin color rather than place of origin.

> The intelligence test . . . soon was used to "prove" that some groups were intellectually superior.

One prominent example of scientific racism was the large intelligence testing program for the US Army in World War I, in which psychologists tested nearly two million soldiers. According to psychologist Robert Yerkes, leader of the testing effort, the most intelligent soldiers were those of northern European or Anglo-Saxon descent, while recent immigrants or their offspring from Italy, Greece, or Eastern Europe were not as smart.

The army psychologists extended their interpretation of the results to indicate that African Americans were the least intelligent, with scores on average equivalent to an eleven-year-old's. Psychologists went further with the African American results by checking scores based on skin color to determine if being of partial European descent made a difference in scores. Those African Americans with the lightest skin color had the highest scores.

Here is an excerpt from the official 1921 report (page 531): "Two battalions were classified as lighter or darker on the basis of offhand inspection. Two other battalions were classified as black, brown, and yellow on the basis of skin color. The median score of the 'black' Negroes was 39, that of the 'yellow' was 59; while that of the 'brown' Negroes fell between these values."

These were the beliefs of the dominant social group; but within a few years a new cohort of African American psychologists and educators would successfully challenge these results. Beginning in the 1920s with the work of both African American and Latino/a psychologists, as well as the work of such psychologists as Otto Klineberg and Thomas Russell Garth, the notion of intellectual racial superiority was shown to be without basis.

SEE ALSO The Doll Studies: Racism and Child Self-Image (1943), Martin Luther King Jr., Psychology, and Social Justice (1967), The BITCH Test (1970), Stereotype Threat (1995)

PROJECTIVE TESTS:
THE RORSCHACH INKBLOTS

Hermann Rorschach (1884–1922)

A NEW KIND OF PSYCHOLOGICAL TEST dominated the period from the early 1920s until the 1960s. So-called projective tests were developed in the hopes of eliciting unconscious material from patients. Sigmund Freud

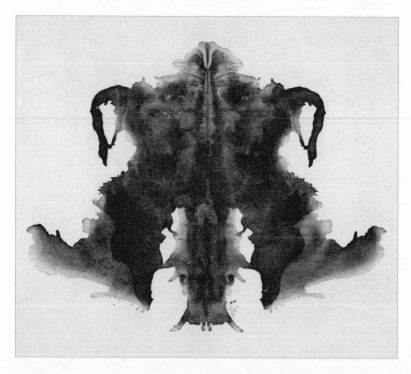

Card four of the ten official Rorschach inkblot cards. The Rorschach Projective Technique analyzes a patient's responses to a series of abstract inkblots, and is one of the most widely used psychiatric assessment tools in the United States.

had theorized that psychologically relevant material was often suppressed because it contained wishes and impulses that were socially unacceptable, yet it was just this material that held the key to unlocking the psyche and bringing relief.

A projective test uses ambiguous stimuli in the form of images, words, or objects to which the client is asked to respond. For example, a patient may be asked to complete this sentence stem: "When I was a child my father . . ." No diagnosis or therapy was offered on the basis of one response, but when numerous such ambiguous stimuli are presented, a person's psychological issues emerge in the pattern of responses.

The first formal projective test is the eponymously named Rorschach Projective Technique, first published in 1921. Swiss psychiatrist Hermann Rorschach, nicknamed "Inkblot" as a child, was influenced by both Freud and Carl Jung and used his childhood fascination with inkblots to create a test to use with mental patients. It was brought to the United States in the 1920s and quickly became the most widely used assessment tool in psychiatric settings. New projective tests soon emerged, such as the Thematic Apperception Test (TAT), the Dramatic Productions Test, and the Szondi, the Blacky, and the Lowenfeld Mosaic tests, to name only a few of hundreds.

All of these tests assumed that the most important determinants of behavior had their origins in the unconscious. As TAT codeveloper Henry Murray was fond of saying, "Every man knows something about himself which he is willing to tell; he knows something about himself that he is not willing to tell; and there is something about himself that he doesn't know and can't tell."

SEE ALSO Psychoanalysis: The Talking Cure (1899), Thematic Apperception Test: Our Stories and Our Personality (1935)

1922

FEMININE PSYCHOLOGY

Karen Horney (1885–1952)

KAREN DANIELSEN HORNEY experienced significant personal and professional setbacks in life, yet she offered important insights into how we can deal with our anxieties. Her work on psychology from a feminine perspective was among the first to challenge Sigmund Freud's ideas about the inadequacy of women's psychological development. She published a series of articles on female psychology from 1922 to 1937; these papers were later collected and published as *Feminine Psychology* in 1967.

> [Karen Horney] argued that what hindered women psychologically was not some fundamental flaw in their physical makeup but the social constraints placed on them.

Horney grew up in Hamburg, Germany, in a home whose dynamics shaped her career. Both parents favored her brother, who was abusive toward Karen. She was not encouraged to pursue her dream to become a physician. After medical school, Karen trained as a psychoanalyst and worked in Berlin until 1932, when she moved to Chicago. Two years later, she moved to New York, where she founded her own institute and journal.

Early in her professional practice she grew dissatisfied with some aspects of Freudian theory, particularly Freud's contention that it was impossible for women to experience full psychological development, which led them to envy male development as symbolized by the penis. She argued that what hindered women psychologically was not some fundamental flaw in their physical makeup but the social constraints placed on them. Because of these constraints, both healthy and neurotic women tended to overvalue love because of their economic and social dependence on men.

The themes of intimate and familial relationships continued to figure prominently in Horney's writing. She wrote that in many families, children develop a basic anxiety because they feel unsafe, unvalued, and unloved. In response they try to reduce anxiety by developing ways to defend themselves either through love, power, or detachment. Healthy adults demonstrate a flexible use of these three strategies, but too often, one or more of the strategies becomes exaggerated. Those who exaggerate love may become compliant, seeking to counter anxiety by pursuing approval and making themselves overly dependent on others. This, Horney argued, was especially problematic for women and hindered their psychological development.

SEE ALSO Psychoanalysis: The Talking Cure (1899), Cultural Relativism: Culture, Sex, and Coming of Age (1928), Humanistic Psychology (1961)

CAPGRAS SYNDROME

Joseph Capgras (1873–1950)

CAPGRAS SYNDROME is an unusual brain disorder in which sufferers become convinced that the people in their lives are not who they appear to be. In one bizarre case, a man, convinced that a robot had replaced his father, decapitated him in order to locate the batteries and recover the microfilms he knew were inside. A person with Capgras syndrome will insist that there are subtle differences between a real friend or family member and the supposed impostor. Since others do not detect these (imagined) differences, it confuses the Capgras patient and may lead to paranoid suspicions about why no one else will acknowledge the substitution—thus the unfortunate outcome described above.

After the syndrome was first described, by the French psychiatrist Joseph Capgras in 1923, the most common explanations for it were often psychoanalytic, such as repressed anger or sexual desire toward the "double"; often, the patient was thought to be schizophrenic. However, the Capgras sufferer is not delusional; rather, something has happened in the way information about other people is processed in the brain.

Recent research suggests that Capgras syndrome results from a disconnect between the parts of the brain that help us recognize others. One brain system, thought to be in the prefrontal cortex, deals with factual knowledge—"your features are precisely the same as my wife's"—while another part of the brain, the limbic system, provides emotional information—"you look like my wife, but I do not have a warm emotional feeling toward you."

The disorder underlines the important connection between our thoughts and our emotions. Many times we can acknowledge what the facts are in a situation, but our emotional evaluation of those facts may lead us to a different conclusion from the one the facts alone would suggest.

A photograph by Polish American artist and mask designer Władysław T. Benda of a man wearing a lifelike but off-kilter mask, 1925; individuals suffering from Capgras syndrome believe that the people in their lives are not who they appear to be.

SEE ALSO The Case of H. M. (1953)

SEEING THE BRAIN AT WORK

Hans Berger (1873–1941),
Raymond Damadian (b. 1936)

ONE OF THE GREATEST ADVANCES in neuroscience and psychology has been the development since the 1950s of increasingly refined brain imaging technologies. Through the intelligent use of these techniques, scientists now know more about the links between brain and behavior than ever before.

Hans Berger invented the electroencephalogram (EEG) in 1924, and it became widely used to measure activity in the human brain. It remains

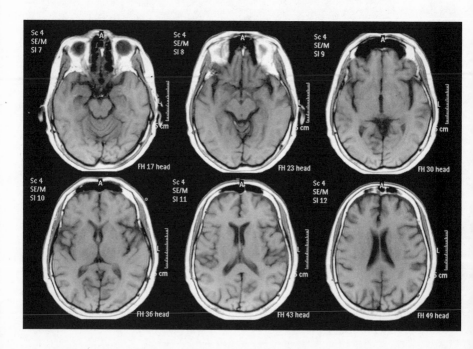

MRI images of the brain identify diseased brain tissue, in addition to tracking neuronal activity.

a useful tool for telling scientists when, but not where, activity takes place. Then, in 1963, the computed tomography (CT) scan was patented. Computerized axial tomography (CAT) uses a series of X-ray "slices," or pictures, to reconstruct a detailed image of a part of the brain. It has been very useful as a diagnostic tool in locating tumors and abnormalities.

In 1972, after almost two decades of research, medical practitioner Raymond Damadian patented the first magnetic resonance imaging (MRI) machine, which he envisioned as a tool for detecting cancerous cells. The technology has continued to be refined, and today an MRI detects changes in the alignment of the nuclei of brain cells when a radio wave is passed through the brain. The results are analyzed by a computer, which then constructs a 3-D image that shows healthy and diseased tissue, as well as blood clots and other pathologies.

Brain activity can be detected by a positron emission tomography (PET) scan, which tracks injected radioactive glucose as it is used in the brain. The brain cells that are most active will show the greatest use of the glucose.

The most powerful technique now in use is the functional MRI (f MRI), which tracks the use of oxygen in the blood. When neurons are active, they use more oxygen, thus activity in any one part of the brain can be tracked as it happens. Neuroscientists now rely extensively on f MRI images to study almost every facet of human brain functioning.

SEE ALSO Neuroplasticity (1948), Right Brain, Left Brain (1962), The BRAIN Initiative (2013)

SOMATOTYPES: DOES BODY SHAPE REFLECT OUR PERSONALITY?

Cesare Lombroso (1835–1909), Ernst Kretschmer (1888–1964), William H. Sheldon (1898–1977), George Draper (1880–1959)

THE BELIEF THAT BODY TYPE, or somatotype, is linked to character or personality and life outcomes is ancient. The *doshas* of Ayurvedic medicine, dating from at least five thousand years ago, represent one version of this belief, but theories and practices based on the belief diminished in Western societies with the ascent of modern science. However, in the nineteenth century, Italian physician and criminologist Cesare Lombroso revived the idea in application to criminal types, and by the early years of the twentieth century some physicians and psychologists had developed new variants of the theory and sought to apply it in new ways.

After the defeat of Germany in World War I, many of that nation's elite blamed technology and mechanistic science for Germany's problems and sought holistic or organismic alternatives in medicine and psychology. Psychiatrist Ernst Kretschmer developed a somatotype approach to mental and physical health that linked inherited personality types (e.g., schizothymic and cyclothymic) with three body types: stocky, thin, and athletic. His book describing the theory was published in English as *Physique and Character* (1925).

In the United States, physician George Draper at New York's Columbia-Presbyterian Hospital (President Franklin D. Roosevelt's personal physician) used a constitutional, body-type approach in his research on the role of psychological factors in health and disease. Draper's model included four panels of personality—morphology, physiology, psychology, and immunity—that together "determine the individual's reaction, successful or unsuccessful, to the stress of environment."

William H. Sheldon, with degrees in both medicine and psychology, developed what is probably the best-known theory relating body type and personality. He proposed three main body types, each with unique personality characteristics. The *endomorph* is stocky, with an extroverted personality; the *mesomorph* is also an extrovert, but with an athletic, muscular build; and the *ectomorph* is thin, often tall, introverted, inhibited, and artistic.

William H. Sheldon . . . proposed three main body types, each with unique personality characteristics.

Although somatotype theories have fallen out of favor among scientists, there still remain expressions of this belief in popular culture, such as the stereotype of the jolly fat person.

SEE ALSO Phrenology (1832)

CULTURAL RELATIVISM: CULTURE, SEX, AND COMING OF AGE

Margaret Mead (1901–78)

MARGARET MEAD was a proponent of cultural relativism, or the idea that all cultures must be understood on their own terms, with reference to local context rather than universal context. Much of her fieldwork was designed to understand cultural variations in developmental experiences such as adolescence, sex roles, and attitudes toward marriage and education. Although she was an anthropologist, she utilized psychological theories to help her understand culture.

She was certainly the best-known cultural anthropologist of the twentieth century. Her books, including *Coming of Age in Samoa* (1928), *Sex and Temperament in Three Primitive Societies* (1935), and *And Keep Your Powder Dry* (1942), have become enduring classics. In her lifetime, Mead was a true public intellectual, writing and commenting on both social and scientific issues. A student of Franz Boas, who developed the field of cultural anthropology, she received her PhD from Columbia University in New York City. She and her collaborator Ruth Benedict were both members of the Culture and Personality movement that developed in the 1930s.

In *Coming of Age in Samoa*, Mead showed how individual psychological development is shaped by the demands of the local cultural context. Thus, adolescents will vary in such domains as sexual development, with some cultures expecting sexual interaction at earlier ages. Her book on the Manus tribal group, *Growing Up in New Guinea* (1930), countered the older idea that so-called primitive peoples are like children. The message of both books was that human psychological and social development will vary according to culture rather than follow a consistent universal pattern. Her work was one of the first cross-cultural studies of human development.

While much of her work centered on "primitive" societies, Mead's contribution to American culture is undeniable. She shed light on the long-standing nature vs. nurture debate, popularized anthropology, and expounded on American national character. With her controversial views on sex roles, she was also at the forefront of the US women's movement.

Margaret Mead, who came into the public eye with her study *Coming of Age in Samoa*, peruses a psychology book in a press photograph, c. 1935.

SEE ALSO Nature vs. Nurture (1874), Western Cultural Bias: The Torres Straits Expedition (1898), Culture Determines What Counts as Mental Illness (1904), Sex Roles (1944)

THE SKINNER CHAMBER

B. F. Skinner (1904–90)

B. F. Skinner, c. 1960, placing a pigeon in an operant chamber—popularly known as the "Skinner box"—the standard laboratory apparatus for several generations of behavioral psychologists.

B. F. SKINNER made a science and a technology out of the age-old truth that living creatures, including humans, will work for rewards. He worked with rats and pigeons for many years in strictly controlled laboratory conditions to show how consequences shape behavior; he called his approach operant conditioning and his philosophy of science radical behaviorism. (The term *operant* refers to the organisms' operations on their environments to produce consequences.) Skinner demonstrated that these consequences exerted powerful effects on behavior, and he gave new meanings to words in common use, such as *reinforcement* and *punishment*, to describe these effects. Skinner was able to show that these principles reached into every corner of life.

Skinner was as much an inventor as scientist. Since childhood he had created apparatuses to perform many household tasks. Once he enrolled in graduate school at Harvard in 1928, after his self-confessed failure as a novelist, he quickly embarked on the task of devising equipment to study the phenomena he was interested in.

In 1930, while studying rats' responses to food, he came up with his most famous invention—the operant chamber, popularly known as the Skinner box. Refined over the next decade or so, it was a small box with a lever that a rat could press for food, and a cumulative recorder to log the rate of lever strokes. The chamber was refined over the next few years, and once Skinner switched to pigeons, disks replaced the lever for food delivery. Skinner found that he could observe, predict, and control behavior with amazing precision.

By the 1960s, Skinner's principles of operant conditioning moved out of the laboratory and into many real-life settings: they were used to discipline unruly schoolchildren, help people lose weight, control prisoners, and achieve many other practical goals.

SEE ALSO Classical Conditioning: Pavlov's Bell (1903)

REMEMBERING AND FORGETTING

Frederic C. Bartlett (1886–1969)

HOW DOES MEMORY WORK? How do we forget? What is the structure of memory? One of the most important of the early efforts to answer this question was the work of British psychologist Frederic Bartlett, who argued that humans tend to reconstruct events rather than remember what actually happened. Thus culture and the culturally familiar are extremely important.

In his 1932 work *Remembering: A Study in Experimental and Social Psychology*, Bartlett used a naturalistic approach to study memory. Bartlett asked people to read a story and later asked them to recall it upon numerous successive occasions. The story was a Native American folktale, the "War of the Ghosts," which contained several culturally unfamiliar ideas—at least to British readers—about the supernatural. Bartlett found that when asked to recall the story, readers tended to remember only the gist of it and were unable to remember the details, let alone the words. As the subjects retold the story later, the story was reconstructed with more culturally familiar ideas about the supernatural.

Bartlett argued that recall was actually reconstruction, and reconstruction appeared to operate according to some general principles, such as rationalization, or making it more culturally familiar. According to Bartlett, these findings indicated that memory was stored as hierarchically organized, meaningful schemas (although he disliked this word, preferring "pattern" and "organized setting"). The higher levels of memory encoded the gist of the story, and this determined the details recalled at lower levels. Memory was thus active and organized, giving meaning to incoming material in a process Bartlett called effort after meaning.

This work suggested that earlier memory experiments—which had used meaningless stimuli, such as nonsense syllables—were really assessing a different, and atypical, memory process.

A war crew from the Swinomish tribe in a canoe off the coast of Washington State, c. 1924. In the "War of the Ghosts," two young Northwest Native American men encounter a canoe filled with mysterious warriors, whom they accompany to a ghostly battle. Frederic Bartlett found that British readers could not remember the details of this story, and would later reconstruct it with more culturally familiar ideas about the supernatural.

SEE ALSO Descartes on Mind and Body (1637), Forensic Psychology (1902)

ARCHETYPES: TRICKSTER, SAGE, HERO, AND PRIMORDIAL MOTHER

Carl Gustav Jung (1875–1961)

THE THEORIES OF C. G. JUNG were drawn from many sources, including religion, myth, Eastern philosophies, anthropology, psychology, and folklore. Out of these sources, Jung created complex psychology, or depth psychology. Like Sigmund Freud's psychoanalysis, complex psychology assumes a personal psychological unconscious; Jung, however, proposed a collective unconscious, grounded in human evolution, that is fundamental to human psychological functioning. The collective unconscious serves as the universal background that informs and shapes the personal, individual life.

In his 1934 volume *The Archetypes and the Collective Unconscious*, Jung wrote that archetypes are primordial or archaic images that are indigenous to the collective unconscious and help give shape to individual experience. As such, archetypes may take on a variety of symbolic expressions. Jung did not indicate that there were a fixed number of archetypes, but some common examples are the primordial mother, the sage, the trickster, and the hero. Because they are symbols of the human experience over time, archetypes appear in all cultures, although their form and expression will vary in each culture and era. The truth component of myths, religions, and fairy tales lies in their relation to archetypes.

Aspects of individual psychology are also archetypal, Jung argued. The persona (our social face), the animus/anima (male/female principle), the shadow, the ego, and the self are archetypes, but expressed uniquely in each person. The *ego* is the center of human consciousness and provides a sense of continuity in our conscious lives. The *self* is the deepest aspect of human personality and is the central archetype that knits the conscious and unconscious together, providing order and balance among all the psychic elements. The shadow contains the repressed and unfavorable aspects of the personality. For Jung, the goal of psychological development is what he termed *individuation*. In the process of individuation, which becomes more important in midlife and beyond, the challenge is to integrate the ego and the self, thus leading to psychological wholeness and freedom. It is more often a journey than an arrival.

Archetypes are primordial or archaic images that are indigenous to the collective unconscious and help give shape to individual experience.

SEE ALSO Jungian Psychology: Collective Unconscious and Psychological Growth (1913)

ZONE OF PROXIMAL DEVELOPMENT

Lev Vygotsky (1896–1934)

IN THE FIRST DECADE after the 1917 October Revolution, which brought the Bolsheviks to power in Russia, psychology underwent dramatic changes that eventuated in a search for a truly materialist science. It was during this period that the young lawyer turned psychologist Lev Vygotsky came to Moscow, where he developed a multifaceted research program, including an innovative approach to studying children's development, now often referred to as cultural-historical psychology. During the last two years of his life, he formulated the concept of the zone of proximal development.

Vygotsky's research showed that the cultural, social, and historical context of a child's life is critical for the development of psychological functions. He, his colleagues, and students developed an ambitious program of research that encompassed the study of memory and attention; the effects of brain damage on cognitive development, verbal thinking, and practical intelligence; and cross-cultural studies of ethnic minorities. In much of their work, attention was given to the practical application of their results to children's education.

With the term *zone of proximal development*, Vygotsky indicated that it is not enough to measure a child's current mental age; rather, what has to be considered is the child's potential for development—that is, we must seek to discover what more a child can do through interaction with a teacher, a parent, or an older child. In other words, intellectual development is also a social process, and by this Vygotsky meant to indicate that even the highest mental processes have a social or cultural origin.

Unfortunately, Vygotsky died of tuberculosis at the very young age of thirty-eight while still working on his theory of sociocultural development. For a brief period, his ambitious research program was continued by his students and colleagues. Since the 1980s, American psychologist Barbara Rogoff has extended Vygotsky's theory by showing how learning is culturally embedded in a variety of diverse settings.

OPPOSITE: School children in a period of free activity at a school in Reedsville, West Virginia, 1936. Lev Vygotsky's research showed that the cultural, social, and historical context of a child's life is critical for the development of psychological functions.

SEE ALSO Rousseau's Natural Child (1762), Nature vs. Nurture (1874), Binet and Simon: The First Intelligence Test (1905), Ecological Systems Theory (1979)

THEMATIC APPERCEPTION TEST: OUR STORIES AND OUR PERSONALITY

Henry Murray (1893–1988), Christiana Morgan (1897–1967)

CAN WE UNDERSTAND OURSELVES and others through the stories we tell? More than one personality theorist has argued that we can, because human beings are storytelling creatures. One such narrative approach was the psychodynamic theory of psychologist Henry Murray and his partner, Christiana Morgan. Both were convinced that humans are motivated by unconscious factors that shape our personalities. Together they developed one of the most widely used tests of the twentieth century, the Thematic Apperception Test (TAT).

The TAT was first published in 1935, after a graduate student at the Harvard Psychological Clinic reported to Morgan that to pass the time while her young son was ill, she had asked him to tell stories based on pictures in magazines. The stories he told reflected his worries and hopes related to his illness. Morgan realized the possibilities of this approach and developed a set of illustrated cards using her own artwork, redrawn images from magazines, and photographs. Morgan and Murray called their new test the Thematic Apperception Test because they discovered that most people, when asked to tell a story based on illustrations about what has happened and what occurs next, would tell stories based on their own psychological needs and issues. The TAT was refined for several years in the clinic, and the results were used in the case studies reported in the clinic's major book, *Explorations in Personality* (1938).

There is a fascinating backstory to Morgan and Murray's collaboration. They met at a New York social gathering after Murray had become

This illustrated card from the Thematic Apperception Test depicts a woman standing in a doorway; she is holding the door with her left hand as if for support, and covering her downcast face with her right hand. Morgan and Murray found that most people, when asked to tell a story based on one of the TAT illustrations, tell stories based on their own psychological needs and issues.

a physician, but he knew nothing about psychology. Murray and Morgan were married to others when they met; nevertheless they became romantically involved and worked together until Morgan's death. Morgan educated Murray in psychology so well that he became one of the field's most important figures in the twentieth century.

SEE ALSO Projective Tests: The Rorschach Inkblots (1921); *Lives in Progress*: Psychology and the Stories of Our Lives (1952)

PSYCHOSURGERY

Egas Moniz (1874–1955), Walter Freeman (1895–1972)

BECKY AND LUCY fought a lot. Becky would throw her food, have tantrums, and bite Lucy when she was frustrated. She was more than a handful—until she had a new kind of surgery that separated her frontal lobes. Afterward, her behavior changed so much that her surgeon remarked that it was as though Becky had joined a "happiness cult." Becky and Lucy were chimpanzees.

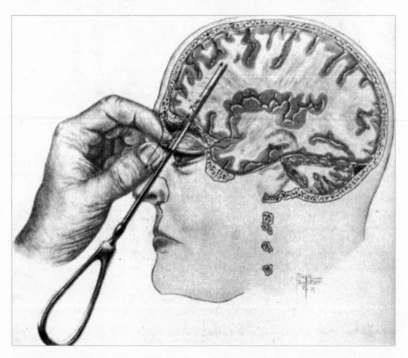

An illustration from Dr. Walter Freeman's book *Psychosurgery* (1950, coauthored with James J. Watts) showing the method for a transorbital or "ice pick" lobotomy, in which an instrument was inserted under the upper eyelid against the top of the eye socket and hammered into the brain.

Yale psychologist Carlyle Jacobsen reported the case of Becky at the 1935 meeting of the International Neurological Congress in London. In the audience was the notable Portuguese neurosurgeon Egas Moniz. Moniz left the meeting convinced that this surgery held great promise. He conducted the first operation of what he was now calling psychosurgery on November 12, 1935, and within three months he had performed twenty psychosurgeries on patients with a variety of serious psychiatric disorders. He claimed that fourteen of the twenty patients either recovered or improved.

Reports of Moniz's new intervention spread rapidly around the world. By 1949, about 5,000 such surgeries, now commonly called lobotomies, were being performed annually in the United States. Neurologist Walter Freeman was by far the most prolific, conducting 3,500 lobotomies from 1936 to 1970. With neurosurgeon James Watts, Freeman pioneered the use of the transorbital lobotomy, in which a surgical spatula was inserted and swept through the frontal lobes. Freeman then developed an in-office procedure in which an ice pick–shaped instrument was inserted into the frontal lobes through the eye socket. The ice pick lobotomy was performed on a number of children, including a four-year-old.

Despite Freeman's advocacy of psychosurgery, its popularity declined in the 1950s and 1960s because of doubts about its efficacy and the introduction of new drugs that promised more effective treatment. However, as late as the early 1970s, figures within the Nixon administration promoted the use of lobotomies as a means to control dissident figures.

SEE ALSO Direct Brain Stimulation and Experiential Hallucinations (1941)

1936

DEFENSE MECHANISMS

Anna Freud (1895–1982)

ANNA FREUD was the sixth and last child of Sigmund Freud and Martha Bernays. She was the only child of Freud's to follow in his footsteps into psychoanalysis. After being analyzed by her father from 1918 to 1922, she developed the field of child psychoanalysis.

As a theorist, Anna Freud was concerned with the development of the ego. Briefly, her father's model of human personality theorizes that at birth, there exists only the id, which is concerned with the fulfillment of basic human needs—eating, sex, and so on. With psychosexual development, the ego emerges as a structure that mediates between the demands of the id and the real world. Finally, with the resolution of the Oedipal conflict, the superego emerges, which is the aspect of personality that reflects standards of right and wrong as expressed by one's parents.

> Anna Freud [used] language that made it possible to understand . . . defense mechanisms.

A healthy personality is possible only if the ego is able to maintain a balance among the competing demands of the id and the superego, but these demands generate anxieties. In order to cope, the ego develops mechanisms to deal with these fears. Over the course of his career, her father had noted these ego defenses, but often without elaboration. Anna Freud brought them together and discussed them in a landmark volume called *The Ego and Mechanisms of Defense* (1936), using language that made it possible to understand them. As a result, many of the terms for these defense mechanisms passed into common usage.

Two examples will serve. Repression is a mechanism that pushes an anxiety-producing idea or event out of conscious awareness. The repressed idea remains active on the unconscious level and may find an outlet, as in a phobia. Sublimation is the mechanism that redirects unacceptable hostile or sexual feelings toward acceptable expression. For example, a very hostile person may turn his or her aggression toward positive ends by becoming a surgeon. Defense mechanisms can play a positive role in helping us keep our balance; however, they may make us neurotic and keep us from effectively dealing with conflicts.

SEE ALSO Anna O.: Converting Psychological Distress into Physical Illness (1880), Psychoanalysis: The Talking Cure (1899)

TURING MACHINE

Alan Turing (1912–54)

ALAN TURING, a young British mathematician, was responsible for one of the great advances that helped make modern digital computing possible and thus laid the groundwork for the later study of artificial intelligence. In 1936, in a paper entitled "On Computable Numbers," Turing proposed a

US Navy version of the bombe device, which was originally developed by Alan Turing and used by British cryptologists against the German cipher machine Enigma–M4 to decipher encrypted messages during World War II.

computational device designed to investigate the limitations of what can be computed, proving that a machine could calculate anything that was quantifiable and offering a workable definition of computation that was used as the basis for developing the modern digital-computer program. In 1937, Turing's hypothetical machine was christened a Turing machine.

Turing used his mathematical skills to help break the German military codes during World War II. He used a computational method modeled on his earlier theoretical work that guided a machine, named the bombe, through nearly all possible number-letter combinations until a comprehensible message was generated. Turing showed how the concept of computation can be expressed in terms of a system of rules.

In her book *Mind as Machine* (2006), researcher Margaret Boden wrote that the significance of the exercise was to show how "abstract machines could be described in a standard logical form, and how they could be used to do elementary computations out of which all standard arithmetical operations could be constructed."

In 1950, Turing asked the question, "Can a machine think?" He devised a thought experiment—the Turing test—in which a human judge has a "conversation" with another person and a machine; the conversation is conducted via a keyboard, and the participants are not visible to one another. The machine has passed the test if the judge cannot tell the difference between the respondents' answers. Although only a thought experiment, the Turing test proved important for later developments in artificial intelligence.

SEE ALSO The First Thinking Machine (1843), Cybernetics, Computers, and the Beginning of Cognitive Science (1943)

1941

DIRECT BRAIN STIMULATION AND EXPERIENTIAL HALLUCINATIONS

Wilder Penfield (1891–1976)

A YOUNG PSYCHOLOGIST is under a surgical tent at the Montreal Neurological Institute. It is 1939, and psychologist Molly Harrower is about to record some of the most interesting data ever provided by brain-surgery patients. Her role is to record verbatim what each one reports. The patients all suffer from epilepsy and have agreed to participate in an innovative procedure devised by American Canadian neurosurgeon Wilder Penfield.

With patients under local anesthetic, Penfield surgically exposed the cortex of the brain; then, using a tiny electrode, he stimulated various parts of the brain. Some spots appeared to be related to the aura that many epileptic patients experience prior to a seizure; these he surgically removed. Areas relevant to movement and sensation yielded the expected experiences when stimulated; for example, patients reported seeing flashes of color when the visual cortex was touched.

When Penfield first reported these findings in 1941, he also indicated that further stimulation of the temporal lobe produced surprising results, including what he called "experiential hallucinations,"

> [Penfield] indicated that further stimulation of the temporal lobe produced surprising results, including . . . "experiential hallucinations."

or psychical discharges. When certain areas in the temporal lobe were touched by the electrode, patients reported hearing songs they had last heard as a child, or they saw a portrayal of some event they may have viewed in a movie. In one famous reenactment, the patient cried out, "I can smell burned toast" when a seizure origin point was stimulated. Penfield thought these hallucinations were accurate flashbacks of the original experience. He also found what he termed "interpretative illusions," which included experiences of déjà vu and perceptual distortions as well as a sense of unreality, euphoria, or dread.

Most of his patients reported these experiences as quite intense, with qualities very different from everyday experiences—more dreamlike than the reality of daily life. Penfield's intention was to help his patients gain relief through surgical intervention. But he found that cortical stimulation also had implications for localization of brain function and for memory.

In 1951, he and Canadian neurologist Herbert Jasper published the landmark work *Epilepsy and the Functional Anatomy of the Human Brain*, in which Penfield created sensorimotor maps of the brain's cortex, the soon-to-be famous cortical homunculus. This work has had profound impact on our understanding of how brain functions are localized.

SEE ALSO Where Brain Functions Are Localized (1861), Seeing the Brain at Work (1924), Right Brain, Left Brain (1962)

CYBERNETICS, COMPUTERS, AND THE BEGINNING OF COGNITIVE SCIENCE

Norbert Wiener (1894–1964)

THE TERM CYBERNETICS (from the ancient Greek *kybernētēs*, for *pilot* or *steer*) was coined in 1834 by the French physicist and mathematician André-Marie Ampère to describe the "sciences" of government. But American mathematician Norbert Wiener was the first to use the word to describe the study of self-regulating systems.

During World War II, Wiener was working on a military project on the guidance and control of aircraft fire when he came to the conclusion that to solve the self-correcting tracking problem, he would need to employ the notion of feedback, both in the plane and in the human gunner, as an integrated system. In 1943, his scholarly paper "Behavior, Purpose, and Teleology" brought together ideas from physiology, behavioral psychology, and engineering to describe a cybernetic organism, or one that was both man and machine. This paper became the manifesto for cybernetics and led to a series of annual conferences that were crucial for the postwar development of what is now referred to as cognitive science.

> Three concepts are crucial in cybernetic theory: feedback, information, and purpose.

From the beginning, cybernetics was an interdisciplinary research area in which psychologists, biologists, mathematicians, engineers, and others studied the interaction of brain and machine. Three concepts are crucial in cybernetic theory: feedback, information, and purpose. Feedback relies on an information flow about the organism or machine in order to regulate the activity of the organism or machine. Self-regulating systems have a purpose or goal, such as maintaining a constant temperature.

An event that took place at the Macy conference of 1952 illustrates these concepts. Information theorist Claude Shannon brought along a mechanical maze-running rat equipped with an electrical contact "finger," which it used to detect the walls of a maze made up of twenty-five squares. Using feedback from these contacts and programming that allowed it to avoid blind alleys, the rat successfully navigated the maze.

The ways these ideas were deployed in combination with information theory to encompass both human systems (biological and social) and machine systems led to a period of innovative scientific discovery. With parallel developments in computer science and neuroscience, the new field of cognitive science was born, which has gradually changed the field of psychology.

SEE ALSO The First Thinking Machine (1843), Turing Machine (1937)

THE DOLL STUDIES:
RACISM AND CHILD SELF-IMAGE

Kenneth B. Clark (1914–2005), Mamie Phipps Clark (1917–83)

Kenneth B. Clark and Mamie Phipps Clark, c. 1955.

ON MAY 17, 1954, in the case of *Brown v. Board of Education of Topeka*, the US Supreme Court declared racial segregation in public schools to be unconstitutional. In their unanimous opinion, the justices cited evidence from social-science research to support their decision. A critical part of that evidence was the "doll studies" of Mamie and Kenneth Clark.

The two met at Howard University in Washington, D.C., in 1934. Kenneth soon graduated and moved to Columbia University. They were secretly married during Mamie's senior year, and she continued at Howard University for her master's degree, completing it in 1939. In her master's thesis she explored how racial identity formed in Black preschool children. After completing her degree, Mamie joined Kenneth at Columbia, where they continued their research on racial identity. They added new materials to the study, including dolls of different skin colors (two white and two Black). In each school, the children were presented with the dolls and asked to pick one in response to requests such as "Give me the doll that you like to play with," "Give me the doll that is a nice doll," "Give me the doll that looks bad," and "Give me the doll that is a nice color." They found that many African American children equated good qualities with white dolls and attributed negative qualities to the darker colored dolls, even though they knew themselves to be African American. The Clarks completed their research in 1943.

The results were disturbing, but with the Clarks' permission, the National Association for the Advancement of Colored People used the doll studies as evidence of the psychological damage of racial segregation in *Brown*. The decision was a bright and shining moment in American history, though many challenges lay ahead. Mamie and Kenneth Clark showed the power of psychological science in the cause of social justice.

SEE ALSO Identity Crisis (1950), Contact Hypothesis or How to Reduce Racism and Bias (1954), Stereotype Threat (1995)

1943

MASLOW CREATES
THE HIERARCHY OF NEEDS

Abraham Maslow (1908–70)

AS A YOUNG PSYCHOLOGIST in New York City, Abraham Maslow became a junior member of an intellectually rich group that was interested in questions of culture and personality. Maslow grew up in an unhappy home in Brooklyn and was determined to make his life better. Intellectually stimulated by his colleagues, in 1943 he proposed a new theory of what motivates humans and forms our personalities.

He suggested that our motivation is related to the satisfaction of our needs, which are hierarchically related to one another. Thus, our most basic set of requirements is physiological: we must eat to survive. Once this is met, we then are motivated to be safe; then we have strong wishes to belong and to love and be loved; and once those are met, we then want to find esteem and respect from others. The highest need, one that we can focus on when all the others are met, is the desire for self-actualization, a term he borrowed from neurologist Kurt Goldstein. Maslow wrote that self-actualization meant striving to be all that one is capable of being.

Maslow argued that psychology was overly concerned with human deficits and problems and that we knew too little about human potential. To address this, he studied people he viewed as self-actualizing, such as Abraham Lincoln, Albert Einstein, and Eleanor Roosevelt. People who are in the process of self-actualizing, he wrote, are spontaneous, creative, empathic with others, and self-directed. Self-actualizing people are likely to have "peak experiences," or times when awareness is heightened and they experience awe and even ecstasy.

Maslow's theory emphasized personal growth, becoming, and the value of heightened subjectivity. With his colleagues he created a "third force" in psychology that emphasizes the positive side of human nature and foreshadowed the later development of positive psychology.

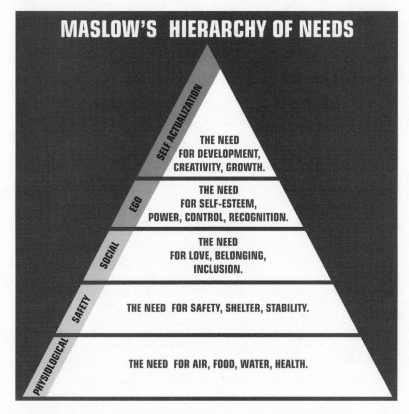

MASLOW'S HIERARCHY OF NEEDS

SELF ACTUALIZATION — THE NEED FOR DEVELOPMENT, CREATIVITY, GROWTH.

EGO — THE NEED FOR SELF-ESTEEM, POWER, CONTROL, RECOGNITION.

SOCIAL — THE NEED FOR LOVE, BELONGING, INCLUSION.

SAFETY — THE NEED FOR SAFETY, SHELTER, STABILITY.

PHYSIOLOGICAL — THE NEED FOR AIR, FOOD, WATER, HEALTH.

According to Abraham Maslow's hierarchy—often represented in a pyramid diagram—the highest need, pursued when all others have been met, is self-actualization. This involves the development of creativity, spontaneity, and empathy, as well as "peak experiences" of heightened awareness or ecstasy.

SEE ALSO Cultural Relativism: Culture, Sex, and Coming of Age (1928), Humanistic Psychology (1961), Positive Psychology (2000)

AUTISM

Leo Kanner (1894–1981),
Bruno Bettelheim (1903–90),
Ole Ivar Lovaas (1927–2010)

ANDRE IS FOUR YEARS OLD but seldom speaks. When touched by his mother, he turns away and never returns affection. Andre does not make eye contact and appears uncomfortable when others look at him. He has a few behaviors that he repeats over and over. His caregivers have to watch carefully, as he is prone to engage in self-harming behaviors, such as beating his head on the floor.

The above is a fictional case study of a child with autism. In the United States alone, the official government estimate is that one in eighty-eight children suffers from autism or autism spectrum disorder. It is a pervasive developmental disorder, meaning it affects nearly every aspect of a person's life, and it is five times more common among boys than girls. Autism is usually detected by the time a child is two and a half years old, but signs may appear in the first few weeks of life. It is not clear what causes autism. There does not appear to be one single cause of autism, but research has found atypical brain structures in children with autism, while other research indicates a significant genetic role.

> [Autism] is a pervasive developmental disorder, meaning it affects nearly every aspect of a person's life.

Leo Kanner, a psychiatrist at Johns Hopkins University, was the first person to describe autism in a landmark 1943 paper. He offered the view that autism was somehow connected to mothers who were not warm and responsive to the child. This idea was picked up by other mental health providers, including the psychoanalyst Bruno Bettelheim. Bettelheim elaborated a theory of autism based on what he called the "refrigerator mother." The term refers to a mother who withholds affection from the child and acts as though she does not want the child to exist. This set of actions leads the child to withdraw into an internal psychological shell in self-defense. The refrigerator mother hypothesis has been widely discredited and now appears as an artifact of negative bias based on gender discrimination.

Later, behavioral therapists such as Norwegian American psychologist Ole Ivar Lovaas demonstrated that behavioral techniques, such as positive reinforcement, could be used to teach autistic children to speak and engage in social interactions. Animal scientist Temple Grandin is an example of a prominent, well-known, and successful person with autism.

SEE ALSO Bleuler Initiates the Modern Study of the Schizophrenias (1908), The Skinner Chamber (1930), Theory of Mind (1978)

SEX ROLES

Georgene Seward (1902–92)

THE TERMS *SEX ROLES* and, since the 1970s, *gender roles* have been used by psychologists and other social scientists to refer to the socially desig-nated behaviors, attitudes, and activities that have been deemed appropriate for men and women. Sex roles have been a source of research interest for psychologists since the late 1800s. At that time, female psychologists like Helen Thompson Woolley and Leta Hollingworth published empirical studies to challenge beliefs about male and female differences that contrib-uted to the sex-role stereotypes of the time.

In the post–World War II period, interest in sex roles intensified because many women had taken on nontraditional employment during the war. In 1944, psychologist Georgene Seward chaired a committee on Sex Roles in Postwar Society for the Society for the Psychological Study of Social Issues. She called for a radical restructuring of traditional sex roles in the postwar reconstruction so that men and women could participate equally in the world of work. Her call was supported by an analysis of the cultural conflict faced by women under contemporary gender arrangements and was followed by a 1946 book, *Sex and the Social Order*.

When the women's movement of the late 1960s and 1970s gained momen-tum, feminist psychologists conducted studies to investigate the effects of sex-role stereotypes on attitudes and behaviors in a wide variety of domains. In one line of research, the relationship between sex-role stereotypes and perceptions of mental health was assessed. Some results showed that while mentally healthy men were described as stereotypically masculine and mentally healthy women were described as feminine, a healthy adult (sex unspecified) was described more often as having masculine traits. In 1975, the journal *Sex Roles* was established to publish sociological and psychological research on a wide range of gender issues.

Three aviation machinist mates work on a training plane at Naval Air Station Jacksonville, in Florida, 1944. The movement toward equal-opportunity employment for men and women that began during World War II intensified after the war, with many women assuming occupations traditionally held by men.

SEE ALSO Variability Hypothesis: Gender and Genius (1914), Friedan's *The Feminine Mystique* (1963)

LOGOTHERAPY
AND THE
SEARCH FOR MEANING

Viktor Frankl (1905–97)

IN 1942, AUSTRIAN NEUROLOGIST and psychiatrist Viktor Frankl, his wife, his parents, and his siblings were sent to Nazi concentration camps; only he and one sister survived. Frankl spent time in four different camps, including Auschwitz and Dachau. Like most other people who spent time in concentration camps, Frankl experienced many horrors and saw firsthand how inhumane humans can be. He also experienced and observed great compassion and generosity in the camps.

Despite it all, Frankl emerged from the camps with a deep understanding of what is most important to humans. Based on his experiences, he believed that the basic quest of human existence is a search for meaning. His most famous and widely read book, *Man's Search for Meaning* (1962), was originally published in Austria in 1946. (The German title was *Ein Psycholog erlebt das Konzentrationslager*, or *A Psychologist Experiences the Concentration Camp*; the first English-language edition, published in 1959, was entitled *From Death-Camp to Existentialism*.) To date, the book has sold more than twelve million copies.

Frankl was educated in Vienna, earning his medical diploma from the University of Vienna. During this period he was influenced by the psychoanalysts Sigmund Freud and Wilhelm Reich. His wartime experiences led to the development of a third type of Viennese psychotherapy, after psychoanalysis and Alfred Adler's individual psychology. He labeled his existential approach *logotherapy*, or meaning (*logos*) therapy. There are three basic principles in logotherapy: meaning is the most basic desire for humans; there is always meaning to be found in life, no matter how difficult the circumstances; and we are free to find meaning.

We can find meaning in three primary ways: we can make meaning through what we do; we can find meaning through our relationships with others; and meaning can come through our attitude toward unavoidable suffering. Frankl further argued that while suffering is unavoidable, we can transform human tragedy into something that gives meaning to our lives. Frankl believed that logotherapy is a positive force not because it changes our situation but because it helps us change our attitude toward life.

> [Frankl] argued that while suffering is unavoidable, we can transform human tragedy into something that gives meaning to our lives.

SEE ALSO Psychoanalysis: The Talking Cure (1899), Rogers's Client-Centered Therapy (1947), Cognitive Therapy (1955)

1947

ROGERS'S
CLIENT-CENTERED
THERAPY

Carl R. Rogers (1902–87)

AS PART OF THE "THIRD FORCE" of humanistic psychology that arose in American psychology in the twenty-five years after the end of World War II, Carl Rogers's client-centered (or, later, person-centered) therapy was influential in developing modern psychotherapy.

Rogers grew up quite religious and was a theology student before switching to psychology. Early in his career, his therapeutic work with children led him to posit that a nurturing and positive environment was critical for healthy psychological development. Rogers meticulously studied the therapeutic process and detected what he said were the critical therapist variables: the provision of empathy, congruence, genuineness, and unconditional positive regard. He argued that each of us has an inner capacity to know what positively helps us, but this inner capacity can become obscured by obstacles in daily life. For example, when significant others make their love and acceptance conditional upon living and acting in certain ways, these terms of worth can block our psychological growth. The job of the

> Rogers [detected] the critical therapist variables: the provision of empathy, congruence, genuineness, and unconditional positive regard.

therapist is to create a therapeutic relationship in which such conditions of worth are eliminated and the person can recover this innate capacity toward growth.

Rogers articulated the basic principles of client-centered therapy in 1947 and then spent many years investigating the application of the principles in actual clinical cases. The influence of client-centered therapy has been considerable, even though it is rarely practiced in its original form today. Psychotherapy research has revealed that there are common factors that must be present for any type of therapy to work. Not surprisingly, perhaps, these factors are very much like what Rogers described: almost all therapists today are trained to be active listeners, provide appropriate reflections of the client's words, and show empathy as the basis for successful psychotherapy, no matter what other specific techniques may be involved.

Rogers's commitment to helping people become fully functioning and his belief in personhood, self-determination, and human strengths endure in contemporary movements such as positive psychology.

SEE ALSO Maslow Creates the Hierarchy of Needs (1943), Logotherapy and the Search for Meaning (1946), Cognitive Therapy (1955), Humanistic Psychology (1961)

NEUROPLASTICITY

Jerzy Konorski (1903–73)

AT AGE FOUR, LITTLE ALEXANDER speaks English, Spanish, and Greek fluently. Since birth, his father has spoken Spanish and his mother has spoken Greek to him, while he learned English at day care. It is not surprising

Research demonstrates that neural connections in the brain continue to reorganize, based on life experience, well into adulthood.

that Alexander and other children with similar experiences could be so linguistically skilled. Scientists and parents have long observed how quickly children learn. This is because the brain for the first decade or so of life is highly plastic, or malleable, constantly adding new neural connections from experience.

Polish neuroscientist Jerzy Konorski first described this in 1948. It was long thought that this plasticity ended sometime in adolescence and that adult brains were rigid and not capable of major changes. However, research conducted since the 1990s has revealed that, in fact, there is significant plasticity even in the adult brain. As we learn new things, our brains change. When we learn, neural connections involved in the learning are strengthened. Neuroscientists contend that our experiences change both our actual brain structure and how it is organized.

This is possible because within the brain the connections between neurons are constantly changing depending on their usage. The other key concept is the organization of our sensory and motor systems in the cortex. Sensory input from the body is relayed to an area of the brain called the somatosensory strip, while the output—our response—comes from the primary motor cortex.

Research has shown that these areas change and reorganize depending on experience. One study on touch discrimination involving blind volunteers showed that the subjects experienced changes in the visual cortex, which is normally only responsive to visual stimulation in sighted individuals. Scientists now think that the human brain remains plastic throughout life as we constantly adapt to changing experiences.

SEE ALSO Seeing the Brain at Work (1924), Right Brain, Left Brain (1962), The BRAIN Initiative (2013)

1950

THE DISCOVERY OF STRESS

Hans Selye (1907–82)

THE IDEA THAT EMOTIONS play an important role in our physical health is an old one that can be found across time, from the ancient humoral theory to psychosomatic medicine between the World Wars. After immigrating to Montreal, Hungarian endocrinologist Hans Selye developed a model of the relationships among stress, health, and disease that has been called one of the most influential medical theories of the twentieth century.

> [Selye's] model . . . proposed that many events could become stressors that lead to a generalized response in the organism.

While searching for a new hormone in experiments with laboratory rats, Selye found that his rats developed a set of symptoms that included damage to various internal organs, all linked to the hypothalamus-pituitary-adrenal system. He borrowed a term from engineering—stress—to describe the cause of the symptoms. His first complete articulation of the link between stress and illness came in his 1950 book *The Physiology and Pathology of Exposure to Stress*.

For nearly two decades, Selye continued his research on how stress may lead to physical breakdown. His model, the general adaptation syndrome (GAS), proposed that many events could become stressors that lead to a generalized response in the organism as it seeks to adapt to the occurrence and return to normal functioning. The mobilization of the organism's defenses includes a first response from the hypothalamus, which leads to the activation of the adrenal glands, which produce corticoid hormones, which in turn can cause a variety of health problems if the organism is unable to return to its previous balance.

Shortly after Selye's work became known, psychological factors were shown to be critically important in stress and its treatment. Events large and small, from marriage to the everyday hassle of finding a parking space, are now seen as stressful, with implications for both physical and psychological health. A research and treatment industry has arisen around the concept of stress, with psychologists playing a leading role. This industry is fully supported by the public, for whom stress has become linked with almost every disease and malaise. Trauma and negative events that endure often lead to an experience of stress that may benefit from stress-reduction treatments developed by mental health professionals.

SEE ALSO Type A Personality (1959), Psychoneuroimmunology (1975), Mindfulness and Mind-Body Medicine (1993)

IDENTITY CRISIS

Erik Erikson (1902–94)

LAKESHA, AGE THIRTEEN, seems very caught up in herself. She spends a great deal of time thinking about her appearance, wondering about her future, and talking about her activities. She doesn't seem to think anything bad can happen to her. In this, it turns out that she is very similar to most of her same-age peers. The preoccupations of Lakesha and her friends illustrate what German American psychologist Erik Erikson called the identity vs. role confusion stage of psychosocial development.

In his 1950 book *Childhood and Society*, Erikson posited that identity development is the major challenge of adolescence. The demands of this stage of development center on such questions as: Who am I? What am I going to do with my life? How do I fit into my family and my world? For teenagers, these questions and the consequent actions are driven by the need to individuate, or differentiate themselves from their peers and others in their world. Positive identity formation results in a clearer sense of self and provides a platform for the next stage of psychosocial development, which often includes marriage and vocational choice.

There is an interesting biographical aspect to Erikson's emphasis on identity: he did not know his father. He was born in Frankfurt, Germany, to a single mother, who married a Mr. Homburger when Erik was three. Later in childhood, Erikson discovered that Mr. Homburger was not his biological father. Thus he came to adulthood not knowing his own identity. After being trained as a child psychoanalyst by Anna Freud, Erikson married an American woman and emigrated to America during the Nazi period in Germany. After various appointments, he was offered a position in California. On his move there, he decided to settle his identity by becoming his own father: he changed his name from Homburger to Erikson.

Erik Erikson posited that identity development is the major challenge of adolescence.

SEE ALSO Cultural Relativism: Culture, Sex, and Coming of Age (1928), Emerging Adulthood (2004)

CONFORMITY
AND
INDEPENDENCE

Solomon Asch (1907–96)

THE EVENTS OF WORLD WAR II left many thoughtful people worried about the future of human freedom. Many Germans had cooperated with the Nazi regime in the effort to eradicate the Jews and other so-called undesirables. In the United States, massive resources were devoted to propaganda both at home and abroad to assuage fears and generate support for the war effort. For Solomon Asch, a young Jewish professor, these events raised questions about the importance of social influence on our ability to think for ourselves.

After the war, Asch's research turned to consensus building, independence of thought, and conformity, all considered within a social context. He published his first studies on conformity and independence in 1951.

He later explained this body of work in a popular article written in November 1955 for *Scientific American*, titled "Opinions and Social Pressure": "Life in society requires consensus as an indispensable condition. But consensus, to be productive, requires that each individual contribute independently out of his experience and insight. When consensus comes under the dominance of conformity, the social process is polluted and the individual . . . surrenders the powers on which his functioning as a feeling and thinking being depends."

In order to examine the impact of social groups on independence and conformity of thought, Asch recruited male undergraduates for a study of perceptual judgment. Each subject was shown a line of a certain length and asked to choose which of three other lines of varying lengths was the same as the original line (only one matched). Alone, the subjects were almost invariably correct, but when asked in the presence of other students, all of whom were working with Asch, 38 percent chose the incorrect line when the other students did so. Asch varied the conditions in several ways, including having one "partner" who agreed with the subject; this greatly reduced the errors, thus indicating

Social support is important in maintaining independence despite group influence to conform.

that social support is important in maintaining independence despite group influence to conform.

Although the majority of textbooks describe Asch's research as conformity studies, Asch actually found greater support for independent thinking. His results also confirmed his theoretical work on the importance of understanding persons within the context of the social field in which they make judgments.

SEE ALSO Gestalt Psychology: The Whole Is Greater than the Sum of Its Parts (1912), Milgram's Obedience Experiments (1963), Stanford Prison Experiment (1971)

1952

BEES DANCING, EGG-ROLLING BIRDS, AND THE NEW SCIENCE OF ETHOLOGY

Karl R. von Frisch (1886–1982),
Konrad Lorenz (1903–89),
Niko Tinbergen (1907–88)

BEES DANCING, BIRDS ROLLING EGGS, fish making nests, and ducklings imprinting on a human "mother" are all fascinating contributions of a group of scientists who founded the field of ethology after World War II. Ethologists study fish, birds, insects, and mammals within an evolutionary framework; that is, they want to know how animal behavior is organized and what its function is in helping the animal survive.

> Konrad Lorenz wrote about how he could talk to the animals, as Solomon had.

In his book *King Solomon's Ring* (1949), the first English-language edition of which was published in 1952, Austrian scientist Konrad Lorenz wrote about how he could talk to the animals, as Solomon had. His specialty was the relationship of mothers and their offspring. He discovered that if the first object that a duckling sees within a few hours of hatching is a human, then that person becomes the duckling's "mother." The animal has imprinted on the human and will follow him or her anywhere, just as it would a mother duck.

Lorenz's work became very popular in the 1950s and 1960s, as mother-child relationships were of great concern to scientists, politicians, and the public. It was clear that early life experience was crucial in shaping the child.

Dutch ethologist Niko Tinbergen took a different tack by studying a variety of species, but he was best known for his innovative research on the stickleback fish. His research showed the complex chain of events that a male stickleback went through to woo a mate, build a nest, fertilize the roe, and defend the offspring. His message concerned the powerful role of instinct.

It had long been thought that honeybees did not see in color, but ethologist Karl von Frisch convincingly showed that they did. He then extended his work to study the movements of bees after they discovered a source of food. Von Frisch found that bees do different "dances" to indicate the location and distance of food to others in the hive.

These three scientists won the Nobel Prize in physiology or medicine in 1973 because of ethology's important implications for health and human society.

SEE ALSO Darwin's *On the Origin of Species* (1859), Attachment Theory (1969), Traditional Knowledge—Indigenous Psychologies (2019), Climate Crisis Psychology (2020)

LIVES IN PROGRESS: PSYCHOLOGY AND THE STORIES OF OUR LIVES

Robert W. White (1904–2001)

WHAT IS THE BEST WAY to understand a human life? Psychologists have developed tests of intelligence, personality, and ability. When we look at the resulting numbers and scores, do we really know the person who took the test? Psychologist Robert White was not satisfied that human life could be measured by paper and pencil—or by computerized tests. Instead, he spent his career in the study of lives being lived. He published the first edition of his seminal book on the study of individual lives, *Lives in Progress*, in 1952; subsequent editions were published in 1966 and 1975.

> [White] . . . was more interested in peoples' perceptions of key turning points in their lives.

White grew up in New England and was once described as "almost the last of a species of a proper New Englander." He was born into a well-to-do family, was loved by his parents, and was curious about the world. He had a deep passion for the humanities, especially history, but he chose to attend graduate school in psychology. He had the good fortune to enter Harvard's psychology program at just the time that Henry Murray, another unconventional thinker, became the head of the Harvard Psychological Clinic. Over the next few years White was joined by a remarkable group of students and colleagues, many of whom went on to become leaders in personality psychology.

White studied lives in their fullness—the unconscious determinants of present behavior did not concern him. He was more interested in peoples' perceptions of key turning points in their lives: What were their current interests? How had those interests developed or changed over time? How was competence displayed in life? White took individual lives seriously, and it showed in the case studies he produced. He wanted to know about the problems and questions that concerned ordinary people and to hear how they went about addressing them. Many of his case studies were longitudinal reviews of lives over time, so that we could understand where a person had been and where he or she was going. Perhaps no other psychologist has given us such profound insights into human lives and how to study them in all their richness.

SEE ALSO Thematic Apperception Test: Our Stories and Our Personality (1935), Positive Psychology (2000)

THE CASE OF H. M.

Brenda Milner (b. 1918)

HENRY GUSTAV MOLAISON was walking to school one day in 1935 when he was hit by a bicycle. He struck his head hard against the ground and was briefly knocked unconscious. However, when he came to, he seemed to be okay. Some years later Henry began having seizures, perhaps caused by the accident. The seizures grew so severe that in 1953 he underwent an experimental surgery in the hopes of reducing their severity. Parts of his hippocampus (which merges short- and long-term memory) and amygdala (which processes memory) were removed. After a period of recovery, he was able to get a job doing fairly simple tasks. It was at this point that his career as "H. M." began.

As H. M., Henry became perhaps the most famous neurological patient of all time. Psychologist Brenda Milner led a research team that frequently assessed H. M.'s memory and other cognitive abilities. From her work, we now know a great deal about the neurological underpinnings of the fundamental abilities of humans, especially learning and memory. Milner's work with H. M. not only described his peculiar memory deficits, but their collaboration also helped us understand the different types and roles of memory.

H. M. could not remember a conversation once it ended or was interrupted. This reflected his lack of ability to form semantic memories—memories of everyday knowledge or of gaining new knowledge. He could remember many events from the time before his surgery, but not afterward; his short-term memory worked fine as well. Henry was also able to form new procedural memories—that is, memories of how to do things.

The amazing story of H. M. has taught us that different types of memory may be processed in different parts of the brain. But his story also tells us how important memory is for our everyday lives.

Neuropsychologist Brenda Milner at TEDxMcGill in Montreal, 2011; Milner's work with H. M. helped further our understanding of the different types and roles of memory.

SEE ALSO Remembering and Forgetting (1932)

1953

REM AND
THE CYCLES OF SLEEP

Eugene Aserinsky (1921–98),
William C. Dement (1928–2020)

ALTHOUGH ALL WARM-BLOODED MAMMALS dream every night, the laboratory-based study of sleep and dreams dates only from the twentieth century. By the 1930s, brain activity during sleep was measured by the new electroencephalogram (EEG) method, and rhythmic patterns were reported. However, it was not until 1953 that University of Chicago physiology graduate student Eugene Aserinsky identified the brain-wave pattern characterized by rapid movements of the eyes during sleep and correlated it with the state of dreaming. It was another graduate student, Aserinsky's colleague William C. Dement, who then developed the study of rapid eye movement (REM) sleep.

During a normal night's sleep, humans cycle through stages, each with its own characteristic brain activity.

What scientists now know is that, during a normal night's sleep, humans cycle through stages, each with its own characteristic brain activity. In stage one, our brains show an alpha rhythm; we can easily awake in this stage and we often experience vivid images that are not dreams. Our sleep deepens in stage two, indicated by small bursts of brain activity. During stage three, the delta rhythm of slow, large brain waves emerges; when the brain-wave pattern is only delta waves, then we are in our deepest sleep, stage four, which lasts about twenty to thirty minutes. Then lights, camera, action! We move into REM sleep. Our heart rate and breathing quicken, and our brain-wave patterns look like they do when we are awake; our eyes move rapidly back and forth behind our eyelids (hence the name REM). Even though all this activity is going on, it is impossible to move, as our skeletal muscles are paralyzed. The first period of REM is the shortest; with each cycle—and depending on how long one sleeps, there can be as many as four cycles per night—it lengthens.

While we need each stage of sleep, research shows that REM is the most important. It is not clear why this is the case, but it is known that loss of REM sleep leads to compromised immune function. On the positive side, there is evidence that our memories are consolidated during REM.

SEE ALSO *The Interpretation of Dreams* Inaugurates the Century of Psychology (1900), Jungian Psychology: Collective Unconscious and Psychological Growth (1913), Direct Brain Stimulation and Experiential Hallucinations (1941)

1954

PLEASURE AND PAIN

José Manuel Rodríguez Delgado (1915–2011),
James Olds (1922–76)

THE DISCOVERY OF SPECIFIC BRAIN LOCATIONS for pain, rage, and
pleasure astonished both scientists and the public in the 1950s. In 1954,
psychologist James Olds reported the sensational results of his research on
pleasure; in the same year, physiologist José Delgado reported the location
of brain centers that could be stimulated to produce pain and rage. These
developments indicated the possibility of a brave new world of mind and
behavior control through brain control. Delgado eventually proclaimed

the possibility of a "psychocivilized" society through these and other direct brain-control methods.

Prior to their work, it was generally thought that pleasure and pain were not localized in the brain but diffused throughout. Olds inserted very fine electrodes into the brain of a rat and, as he later reported, missed the area of the midbrain he intended to stimulate. Instead, he hit the hypothalamus. He noticed that the rat soon learned to prefer the place in the experimental chamber where the stimulation was received. Olds extended the research as he discovered that rats preferred the electrical shock more than they desired a food reward. Some rats would press a lever five thousand times an hour if they received a shock for each lever press!

Delgado, on the other hand, discovered pain centers that could stop behavior or evoke rage reactions. Whereas Olds's electrodes were connected by wires to the control, Delgado developed a remote-controlled "stimo-receiver" that enabled control of behavior from a distance. Rats, monkeys, cats, humans, and other animals were Delgado's subjects. In a famous demonstration in 1963 in his native Spain, Delgado implanted a stimo-receiver in the brain of a bull and, using the controller, stopped the bull's charge toward him. These discoveries frightened many people, who saw in them the potential for mass control. Yet they have also taught us about the richness and complexity of emotional reactions.

OPPOSITE: Delgado in a bullring in Cordoba, during his famous 1963 demonstration. The physiologist showed that it was possible to stop a bull's charge by simply pressing a button to stimulate the brain's pain centers.

SEE ALSO The Skinner Chamber (1930), Direct Brain Stimulation and Experiential Hallucinations (1941)

CONTACT HYPOTHESIS OR HOW TO REDUCE RACISM AND BIAS

Gordon Allport (1897–1967)

ONE OF THE MOST ENDURING CONCEPTS in American social psychology is the contact hypothesis, which in its simplest form states that, under certain conditions, intergroup contact among groups that are different in some important dimension, such as skin color, ethnicity, or social class can reduce prejudice and produce more positive intergroup attitudes. More than seven hundred scientific studies have examined the concept since noted social psychologist Gordon Allport introduced it in 1954. What gave rise to such a fruitful social-science construct?

Right after the end of World War II, social scientists in New York City sought to demonstrate how their sciences could help solve real-life problems. One of the pressing problems was interracial housing in large urban areas. The war effort had brought many racial and ethnic minorities to large cities to work in factories, yet very little new housing was being constructed. After the war, tensions rose in regard to who would live where, since the usual pattern in America had been segregated housing. Social scientists saw this as an opportunity to do research that would inform policy while also shedding light on how to reduce racial discrimination and improve intergroup relations.

In New York and nearby cities, there was a rise in the number of housing developments that included both Black and white residents. This created a natural laboratory that could help answer questions about contact between different racial groups. Researchers on these integrated projects found that tenants of both races reported a higher number of friendships with members of the other race, and whites had more favorable attitudes toward integrated housing. The researchers concluded that it was the experience of living in close contact with people of other races that led to the attitude change. It was this idea that Allport turned into the apt phrase "the contact hypothesis."

Gordon Allport was one of the social scientists who informed policy on integration in the 1950s, including on the desegregation of schools. This photograph by Thomas J. O'Halloran shows students in an integrated classroom at the Barnard School in Washington, DC, 1955.

SEE ALSO Army Intelligence Tests and Scientific Racism (1921), The Doll Studies: Racism and Child Self-Image (1943), Stereotype Threat (1995)

COGNITIVE THERAPY

Albert Ellis (1913–2007),
Aaron T. Beck (b. 1921)

SINCE THE MID-TWENTIETH CENTURY, cognitive therapies have gained widespread acceptance as the treatment of choice for a variety of psychological problems. In the United States, Albert Ellis, a psychologist who had trained as a psychoanalyst, pioneered the first cognitive therapy, which he called rational emotive behavior therapy (REBT). Ellis initially chose psychoanalysis as a way to understand the psychological dynamics of his childhood and help others unpack the childhood origins of their own unhappiness.

By the early 1950s, however, he grew impatient with the slow pace of analysis and its constant focus on the past. Ellis began to concentrate instead on how people's thoughts and self-statements keep them trapped in their problems. He noted that people "musturbated"; that is, they irrationally focused on "musts," "shoulds," and "oughts." For example, young adults choose the wrong career because they must please their parents, or they engage in constant self-criticism because they should be loved by everyone, and they ought to make the right decisions always.

REBT therapy uses methods such as thought disputation to challenge patients about their false beliefs. It asks questions such as, "Why must you always please your parents?" or "How is it possible that everyone would love you?" Through practice and homework assignments, the client is able to stop acting on irrational beliefs and construct new thought patterns.

A few years after Ellis introduced REBT, Aaron T. "Tim" Beck began publishing his first work on cognitive therapy. Beck, too, had begun his career as a psychoanalyst, but he failed to find research support for some of the key ideas in psychoanalysis. He gradually developed a cognitive approach that teaches patients to identify and challenge automatic but dysfunctional thoughts. Originally developed to treat depression, Beck's cognitive therapy has now been shown to be effective in dealing with a variety of mental disorders, such as anxiety and marital problems.

In developing REBT, psychologist Albert Ellis noted that people irrationally focused on "musts," "shoulds," and "oughts"—for example some young adults choose careers they dislike because they *must* please their parents, they engage in self-criticism because everyone *should* love them, and they feel they *ought* to make certain decisions.

SEE ALSO Psychoanalysis: The Talking Cure (1899), Logotherapy and the Search for Meaning (1946), Rogers's Client-Centered Therapy (1947)

PLACEBO EFFECT

Henry K. Beecher (1904–76)

ONE OF THE MOST STUDIED MEDICAL and psychological phenomena of the twentieth century was the placebo effect. The word placebo comes from the Latin word meaning "to please." It has been defined as any treatment that contains no known or proven active curative agent, such as a prescription pill that is in fact inert, though the patient has been told it will be effective. The beneficial effect of receiving the placebo appears to stem from the expectation of improvement. Placebo effects have been found in the treatment of a wide range of medical and psychological conditions. Modern researchers have concluded that such placebo effects are normal or typical responses to treatment.

Although the placebo effect must surely have existed for millennia, its documented history in Western medicine dates from the eighteenth century. During the nineteenth century, the placebo effect was widely acknowledged as part of the physician's armamentarium. The diverse nostrums prescribed by itinerant healers, phrenologists, and snake-oil salesmen in rural and pioneer America presumably relied on a similar mechanism of treatment to achieve some beneficial results for the patients who used them.

The serious study of placebos and the placebo effect can be dated from the publication of physician Henry K. Beecher's "The Powerful Placebo" in the *Journal of the American Medical Association* (1955). The paper stimulated research that pointed to a psychological role in health and illness—such as Hans Selye's theory on stress or the linkage of coronary heart disease to what came to be called the Type A Personality—and gave a new impetus to the study of mind-body connections in health and disease. The placebo effect is thought to be important enough to be a necessary part of randomized controlled trials of all new medications.

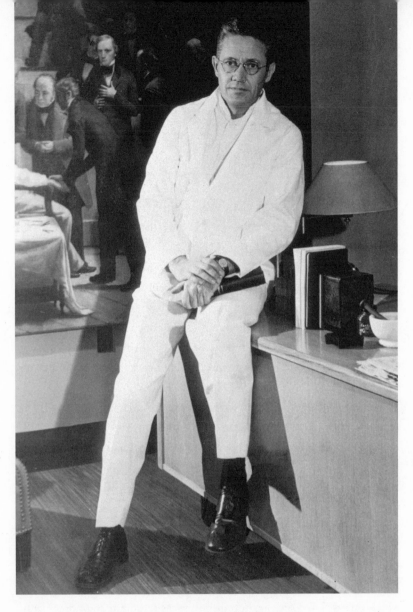

Henry K. Beecher in his office at Harvard Medical School, 1955.

SEE ALSO Mind-Cure (1859), Type A Personality (1959),
Psychoneuroimmunology (1975), Mindfulness and Mind-Body Medicine (1993)

ANTIDEPRESSANT MEDICATIONS

Roland Kuhn (1912–2005)

IN 1952, A DRUG UNDER DEVELOPMENT for use with tuberculosis patients, iproniazid, was found to be effective in treating depression. Approved for use in 1958, it was withdrawn three years later when it was found to cause serious liver damage. In 1955, imipramine was being considered as a treatment for people suffering from schizophrenia at a mental hospital in Switzerland, but the results were not positive. Psychiatrist Roland Kuhn decided to try the drug on forty depressed patients, and the results were all positive. Patients became livelier, their voices were stronger, they were able to effectively communicate, and hypochondriacal complaints all but disappeared. He published his results in 1957.

Imipramine moved to the market under the brand name Tofranil. It was the first of what soon became a family of drugs labeled tricyclics (so named because of their three-ring chemical structure). Tricyclics work by inhibiting the reuptake of the neurotransmitters norepinephrine and, to a lesser degree, serotonin, thus initially making more of them available for use in the brain. There can be unpleasant side effects, however, such as dry mouth, constipation, weight gain, and sexual dysfunction.

Another antidepressant that also works by inhibition was discovered shortly after imipramine. The class of drugs known as monoamine oxidase inhibitors (MAOI) prevents the action of an enzyme, monoamine oxidase, which breaks down such neurotransmitters as serotonin and norepinephrine. MAOI side effects are even more dangerous than those of the tricyclics, so they are seldom prescribed today.

In 1987, a second-generation antidepressant, fluoxetine, with the trade name Prozac was approved for use by the US Food and Drug Administration. Prozac and other drugs like it are selective serotonin reuptake inhibitors (SSRIs). Just as their name implies, they inhibit the reuptake of serotonin in the synapse. The response has been phenomenal: within three years of its release, Prozac was the number-one drug prescribed by psychiatrists, and by 1994 it was the number-two best-selling drug of any kind in the world. It does not have many of the side effects of other antidepressants. Indeed, it is used by millions of people who suffer from no mental disorder at all but who use the drug to enhance their personality, lose weight, or increase their attention spans.

> Within three years of its release, Prozac was the number-one drug prescribed by psychiatrists.

SEE ALSO Bleuler Initiates the Modern Study of the Schizophrenias (1908), Bipolar Disorder and Creativity (1851)

COGNITIVE DISSONANCE: HOW HUMANS MAINTAIN PSYCHOLOGICAL CONSISTENCY

Leon Festinger (1919–89)

A MAJOR SOCIAL-PSYCHOLOGY THEORIST of the twentieth century, Leon Festinger made important contributions to how we manage our sense of self and to how we maintain consistency in our beliefs and attitudes. As a result of his research, the field of American social psychology became increasingly oriented toward internal, cognitive states to explain social phenomena. This was not the case elsewhere in the world. His main contribution to the cognitive turn in social psychology was his often-cited book *A Theory of Cognitive Dissonance* (1957).

> Humans are motivated to reduce dissonance, regain their cognitive balance, and restore the Gestalt.

Festinger grew up in New York City and earned his undergraduate degree at City College of New York, where the psychology department stressed an engagement with real-life applications. He then earned his graduate degrees at the University of Iowa and came under the influence of the Gestalt émigré psychologist Kurt Lewin. After World War II, Festinger worked with Lewin at the Massachusetts Institute of Technology (MIT) as a member of Lewin's innovative Research Center for Group Dynamics. Festinger's work in social psychology owes much to Lewin's Gestalt approach, especially the principle that the organism seeks to maintain a sense of social and cognitive balance.

Cognitive dissonance theory posits three basic assumptions. The first is that cognitions (or beliefs or attitudes) may be related to other beliefs. For example, "I am religious" is related to "I attend church regularly." The second assumption is that related beliefs may be contradictory; this is the basis for the emergence of cognitive dissonance. The third assumption is that humans are motivated to reduce dissonance, regain their cognitive balance, and restore the Gestalt.

When the degree of dissonance is great, as when important beliefs or self-perceptions are involved, we become highly motivated to reduce the dissonance. Festinger suggested that we do this by changing one of the dissonant beliefs or attitudes so that it is consistent with the other important related cognition. For example, you love basketball and you believe you are a very good player, but when you try out for your high school team, you don't make the cut. This creates dissonance that you may try to reduce by telling yourself that basketball isn't so great after all.

SEE ALSO Gestalt Psychology: The Whole Is Greater than the Sum of Its Parts (1912), Conformity and Independence (1951)

HOOKER'S RESEARCH: HOMOSEXUALITY IS NOT AN ILLNESS

Evelyn Hooker (1907–96)

The 1960s "raided premises" police department sign just inside the door at the Stonewall Inn in New York City, which designated it as a location that had been raided for "public morals" offenses. A 1969 police raid here led to the Stonewall riots, a landmark event in the history of LGBTQ rights.

EVELYN GENTRY HOOKER has been hailed as the psychologist who was the forerunner of the gay liberation movement. Conducted almost fifteen years before the 1969 Stonewall Riots in New York City ignited the movement in the United States, her study showing that homosexual men were indistinguishable from heterosexual men in terms of psychological adjustment would prove pivotal in changing both social and scientific attitudes about the "pathology" of homosexuality.

Self-described as "hopelessly heterosexual," Hooker was an instructor at the University of California, Los Angeles, in the early 1950s when she was approached by one of her students, Sam From. Sensing he could trust her, Sam confided that he and many of his friends were homosexual, and he implored her to do a scientific study to prove that they were not abnormal. She agreed, procured a research grant, and, through contacts with homophile organizations, she was able to recruit a sample of thirty homosexual men. She administered interviews and tests, including the Rorschach and the Thematic Apperception Test (TAT), both of which clinicians used widely at the time. She then recruited a matched sample of heterosexual men and administered the same tests. The test protocols for both groups were coded blindly and presented to a group of distinguished clinicians. Each clinician was presented with thirty matched pairs and asked to determine which was the protocol from the homosexual participant. The experts were unable to distinguish the protocols from one another.

Hooker made a presentation of her results at the 1955 meeting of the American Psychological Association and published them shortly thereafter, in 1957. Her work was instrumental in removing homosexuality from the *Diagnostic and Statistical Manual of Mental Disorders* in the 1970s, and she remained an active participant in the gay rights movement throughout her life.

SEE ALSO *Psychopathia Sexualis* (1886), Looping Effects of Human Kinds (1995)

MOTHER LOVE

Harry Harlow (1905–81),
John Bowlby (1907–90),
Mary Ainsworth (1913–99)

RESEARCHERS AT THE PRIMATE LABORATORY at the University of Wisconsin-Madison in the 1950s discovered that young monkeys they had raised in isolation were often unresponsive to stimulation when brought in for intelligence experiments, looking away or becoming despondent. Then researchers noticed that the monkeys clung to the cloth diapers placed in their cages to cushion the cold floors. Building on this observation, lab director Harry Harlow designed experiments intended to shed light on, as he put it, the "origin of the infant's love for his mother."

In the 1950s, Harlow created a series of now-controversial experiments to test his ideas about the importance of bodily contact, affection, and love. He published his first full account of these studies in 1958 in the journal *American Psychologist*. Two wire "mothers"—one bare, one covered in terry cloth—were created, each with a nipple for nursing. In one experiment, eight newborn monkeys were given equal individual access to both mothers, with four being fed by the bare-wire mother and four fed by the terry cloth–covered mother. There were no feeding differences between the two groups—the baby monkeys gained weight and grew regardless of which mother fed them; however, there were important differences in the psychological responses to the mothers. All eight monkeys spent much more of their time with the cloth-covered mother, and the amount only increased as they grew older. The dominant theories of the time predicted that the infants would spend more time with the mother that was the source of food, but Harlow showed that contact comfort was perhaps more important for bonding, attachment, and love.

In further experiments, Harlow found that the soft surrogate mother was an important refuge when the babies were frightened and seemed to serve as a secure base from which the infants could explore their environments. These findings complemented contemporaneous research on attachment by British psychologist John Bowlby and American Canadian psychologist Mary Ainsworth. Truly, love consists of more than nourishment.

Harlow showed that contact comfort was perhaps more important for bonding, attachment, and love.

SEE ALSO Attachment Theory (1969)

1959

TYPE A PERSONALITY

Meyer Friedman (1910–2001), Ray Rosenman (1921–2013)

IN 1959, TWO CARDIOLOGISTS reported their observation that many of their male patients exhibited similar behaviors: while at the doctors' offices, the men were impatient, time-conscious, anxious, driven to achieve, and very focused on work—typical, one might think, of the corporate culture of the day. What alerted Rosenman and Friedman to pay attention to these men's behaviors was that they had to frequently replace their medical-office furniture due to the damage these men inflicted on it. The cardiologists followed the progress of these men in regard to coronary heart disease (CHD) and began to suspect that behavioral and psychological factors were linked to the men's heart problems. The pattern was labeled the type A behavior pattern, and by the early 1970s the construct began to be widely investigated.

This discovery occurred at a time when new attention was being paid to lifestyle and health in American culture. By the 1960s, the primary causes of mortality and disability were CHD, cancer, stroke, and accidents; these diseases were costly in both personal and public ways. Health research was beginning to show that many diseases had important behavioral and psychological components. If unhealthy behaviors could be changed and personality modified, then the nation would benefit. CHD was paradigmatic for the shift to a more holistic view of health and the need for psychological expertise in research and treatment. Type A behaviors caught the public's imagination as a way to think about the relationship between mind and health.

Research initially indicated a link between heart disease and the type A behaviors of time urgency, excessive need to achieve, and anxious hostility. Further research narrowed the behavioral and psychological factors down to just hostility, which is manageable through psychotherapy, thus offering another role for psychologists in the treatment of CHD.

A constant sense of time urgency is one of the key characteristics of the Type A personality.

SEE ALSO The Discovery of Stress (1950), Mindfulness and Mind-Body Medicine (1993)

THE VISUAL CLIFF

Eleanor Jack Gibson (1910–2002), Richard D. Walk (1920–99)

IS OUR ABILITY TO PERCEIVE DEPTH INNATE, or do we learn it by experience? Does its method of movement influence the way an animal perceives the world? In a series of elegant experiments, psychologist Eleanor J. "Jackie" Gibson laid the groundwork for the contemporary science of perceptual development; she is best known for her study of the visual cliff at Cornell University, published as a popular article in *Scientific American* in 1960.

With her colleague Richard D. Walk, she devised an experiment to test whether experience plays a role in depth perception. The near side of the "visual cliff" was a horizontal board painted like a checkerboard, and a flat panel of thick glass was placed on top of it. On the far side of the cliff, a checkerboard floor was placed one foot lower, though the heavy glass continued the entire length, giving it a visual sense of depth, like a cliff.

Gibson and Walk tested whether human infants, as well as the young of several other species, would crawl out onto or cross the visual cliff. The thirty-six human babies tested ranged from six to fourteen months old, all of them crawling. The babies were placed in the center of the board and the mothers called to them from either the "shallow" side or the "deep" side. Most of the babies moved from the center at their mother's call, but only three moved in the direction of the deep side. Many of the infants peered down on the deep side, even patting the glass, but refused to move out onto it. Gibson and Walk concluded that depth perception emerges about the time that babies learn to crawl. Thus experience probably plays only a minor role in depth perception. Research with other animals confirmed that depth perception is linked to the emergence of mobility.

A baby crawls along the top of the "visual cliff" designed by Eleanor Gibson and Richard Walk at Cornell University in 1960.

SEE ALSO Gestalt Psychology: The Whole Is Greater than the Sum of Its Parts (1912)

HUMANISTIC PSYCHOLOGY

Carl R. Rogers (1902–87), Abraham Maslow (1908–70)

A "THIRD FORCE" EMERGED in American psychology in the 1950s and found its first institutional voice in 1961, when the *Journal of Humanistic Psychology* was founded. Humanistic psychology was meant to offer an alternative to psychoanalysis, with its insistence on unconscious sexual and aggressive drives. Humanistic psychology also rejected behaviorism and its depiction of humans as mechanical responders to reinforcement and punishment. It owed much of its inspiration to older phenomenological and existential philosophers whose work focused on the individual's unique experience of the world and the struggle to make a meaningful life. But the new humanistic psychologists rejected the pessimism of European philosophies in favor of an optimistic view of human potential and an innate capacity for psychological growth.

Carl R. Rogers was already well known for his innovative client-centered therapy, with its aims of helping people become fully functioning, authentic individuals. Abraham Maslow had inspired many psychologists with his Hierarchy of Needs and his call to study peak experiences, which were thought to express the highest point of the self-actualizing process. The psychologists who gathered to create the third force had just lived through an era of great conformity whose nadir was McCarthyism. At the same time, America had become an intensely consumerist culture whose highest apparent values were accumulation of goods and aspirations to great wealth. Humanistic psychologists argued that conformity and consumerism had obscured the human ability to know our true needs and hindered us from living authentic lives. Humanistic psychologists suggested turning our attention back to those qualities that make us most human: creativity, agency, free will, intentionality, self-determination, imagination, and values.

During the 1960s, humanistic psychology flourished, especially in the private sphere of the psychotherapist's office, where people learned how to lead meaningful lives. In the public sphere, humanistic psychologists' expressions of human potential and the need for authentic lives resonated with the emerging counterculture.

Hippies cross the street at the corner of Haight and Ashbury Streets in San Francisco, 1967, the epicenter of the counterculture's "Summer of Love." Humanistic psychology flourished during this time.

SEE ALSO Maslow Creates the Hierarchy of Needs (1943), Rogers's Client-Centered Therapy (1947), Flow: The Experience of Optimal Living (1990), Positive Psychology (2000)

RIGHT BRAIN,
LEFT BRAIN

Roger W. Sperry (1913–94)

IN THE EARLY 1960S, brain scientist Roger Sperry began a research program with patients who had severe epilepsy. Some years earlier, neurosurgeons had begun performing operations with such patients in which they severed the corpus callosum, or bridge of nerve fibers that connects the two hemispheres of the brain, in the hope of reducing the severity of seizures. But no one had done research with these patients to determine the full effects of the operation. Most of the patients, in fact, seemed pretty normal in their behavior and personality after the operation and typically experienced relief from the most severe seizures.

Sperry, however, thought that these "split-brain" patients might be able to help us understand our conscious minds. Were the two hemispheres dissimilar in their abilities and functions? If so, what were those distinctions, and what difference might they make? He published his definitive study of the results of severing the corpus callosum, "Cerebral Organization and Behavior," in *Science* in 1962.

Sperry had already conducted similar research with split-brain monkeys and found that the two sides of the brain can function independently. With his human patients, Sperry devised clever ways to deliver a stimulus to one side of the brain, thus eliciting one set of behaviors; the same stimulus delivered to the other side would elicit different results. For example, when shown a dollar sign on the left side and a question mark on the right side, a patient would make a question mark when prompted to draw with his left hand; but when asked what he had just drawn, almost invariably the answer was "a dollar sign." Thus Sperry's research showed the world that we have two minds, each with its own consciousness and with some unique abilities and disabilities. In most people, the left hemisphere is verbal and analytic, while the right hemisphere is nonverbal, or more visual and holistic, and definitely thinks for itself.

The left side of this conceptual illustration depicts an analytical, structured, and logical mind, while the right side depicts a visual, creative mind.

SEE ALSO Where Brain Functions Are Localized (1861), Seeing the Brain at Work (1924)

FRIEDAN'S *THE FEMININE MYSTIQUE*

Betty Friedan (1921–2006)

Leading feminist writer and activist Betty Friedan, photographed c. 1960.

IN 1963, A COLLEGE-EDUCATED JOURNALIST and mother of three published a book that ignited the United States women's movement. In *The Feminine Mystique*, Betty Friedan presented the results of a survey of her undergraduate classmates at Smith College, concluding that most of them had suffered the same fate as she: they had become mired in a postwar snare of expectations around domestic duties and motherhood that left them isolated, unfulfilled, and in despair. She called this the "problem that has no name."

Resonating with thousands of American women, Friedan's arguments drew heavily on psychological themes and theories, including psychoanalysis, which she and many other feminists criticized for its pathologization of women, and humanistic psychology, which she drew upon to justify the need for women's self-actualization and liberation.

Friedan had been a psychology major as an undergraduate at Smith and had considered pursuing graduate studies in the field. Although she did not become a psychologist, her thinking and her writing were heavily influenced by the psychological theories she had learned about and that infused popular culture in this period.

Friedan's critique of postwar America's construction of gender roles was not without its own critics. Some charged that Friedan's concerns were primarily the concerns of middle- and upper-middle-class white women and did not reflect the reality that more and more women were entering the workforce during the time she was writing about. Regardless, many women who read the book cited it as the catalyst that mobilized them into political action by the end of the 1960s. Friedan was one of the founders of the National Organization for Women, served as its first president, and in 1970 helped organize the nationwide Women's Strike for Equality, which drew tens of thousands of women to Fifth Avenue in New York City. It was a vivid demonstration of the broad base and sheer power of the women's movement.

SEE ALSO Variability Hypothesis: Gender and Genius (1914), Sex Roles (1944)

MILGRAM'S
OBEDIENCE EXPERIMENTS

Stanley Milgram (1933–84)

THE QUESTIONS OF CONFORMITY and obedience hung over American social sciences in the years after World War II. Why had so many Germans acquiesced in the Nazi scheme to exterminate the Jews? Many accused Nazi war criminals at the Nuremberg trials had used the defense that they had just been "following orders." In this context, in July 1961—three months after the trial of Holocaust architect Adolf Eichmann had begun in Jerusalem—American psychologist Stanley Milgram at Yale University recruited ordinary members of the local community for a study of "teaching and learning," which he published to great controversy in 1963.

> If the teacher protested that he could not do it, the experimenter refused his attempts to stop.

When the subjects, all of them men, arrived at Milgram's laboratory at Yale, each one was greeted by a scientist and asked to wait a few minutes for another man to arrive; unknown to the subject, the second man was actually in league with Milgram. A rigged drawing always resulted in Milgram's helper taking on the role of "learner." After observing the learner being strapped into a chair with electrodes attached to him, the "teacher" (the new arrival) was instructed to administer shocks each time the learner made a mistake in answer to a question. The teacher then sat in front of shock generator with knobs indicating increasing shock levels between 15 and 450 volts.

Once the experiment began, each time the learner made an error, the teacher pressed the knob to "shock" him. The learner, who was not actually being shocked, responded with moans, cries, screams, and then complete silence as the voltage increased. If the teacher protested that he could not do it, the experimenter refused his attempts to stop, telling him, "You must go on" or "The experiment requires that you continue." Almost 63 percent of the teachers went all the way to the highest voltage, with 360 volts the average amount given.

Were these men (and, later, women) evil and heartless or secret psychopaths? The evidence indicates that these were ordinary men and women. The lesson we learn from this is that any of us might obey and conform just as much as these "teachers" did unless we understand the power of the situation and how we can resist it.

SEE ALSO Conformity and Independence (1951), Stanford Prison Experiment (1971)

HEAD START

Martin Deutsch (1926–2002),
Cynthia Deutsch (b. 1928)

IN 1958, TWO PSYCHOLOGISTS in New York City, Martin and Cynthia Deutsch, opened a new experimental program for preschool-age children in three Harlem school districts. Their aim was to see if children who lived in impoverished conditions would benefit from an enriched environment. The children—Black, white, Hispanic—attended a special class meant to stimulate them socially and cognitively. When the children began school the following year, they did better on many school tasks than similar children who had not had this enriched experience.

A teacher instructs a Head Start class at the Webb School, Washington, DC, 1965.

The Deutsches' program was one of several in this era that attempted to provide social, emotional, and intellectual enrichment programs to poor children. These programs represented a change in thinking from a belief that intellectual ability is fixed at birth to one that emphasized the importance of the environment and stimulation.

Some of the psychological research that gave impetus to this change came from laboratory work on rats. For example, in the 1950s a group of psychologists at the University of California, Berkeley, devised enriched environments for some of their rats. Upon autopsy, brain sections indicated a much richer network of neural connections than in control rats that had only experienced standard laboratory environments.

Psychologist J. McVicker Hunt's research in the late 1950s led him to conclude that experience and the immediate environment are vitally important for intellectual development in children, and other psychologists agreed. In the 1960s, President Lyndon Johnson's War on Poverty brought many psychologists and educators together to create a plan for improving educational opportunities for preschool children. This led to the creation of Head Start, now a national program to help young children from low-income families. Its first program lasted only eight weeks in the summer of 1965. By 1966, it was made part of the regular school year and soon was in place in schools around the country. Since its inception, more than twenty million children have benefited from its programs.

SEE ALSO Ecological Systems Theory (1979)

1966

MASTERS AND JOHNSON'S
HUMAN SEXUAL RESPONSE

William H. Masters (1915–2001),
Virginia E. Johnson (1925–2013)

THE LABORATORY STUDY of human sexuality was the landmark contribution of gynecologist William Masters and psychologist Virginia Johnson. Others had studied sex before them, but their pioneering efforts greatly expanded what was known about sexuality and, perhaps more important, helped create a dynamic field of the scientific study of sexuality. Their first major report of their work was *Human Sexual Response*, published in 1966.

Beginning in the nineteenth century, several scientists and physicians had written about sexual behavior. There were psychiatrist Richard von Krafft-Ebing's studies of sexual pathology, *Psychopathia Sexualis* (1886), and physician Havelock Ellis filled six volumes with detailed accounts of sexuality. In America, pioneering research was conducted by social reformer and criminologist Katherine Bement Davis on college women's sexual behavior; psychiatrist Gilbert Hamilton conducted case studies of married couples' sex lives in New York City during the late 1920s; and, of course, Alfred Kinsey had written two volumes on sexual behavior that were based on extensive interviews during the 1930s and 1940s.

The laboratory setting made Masters and Johnson's research possible. By adapting extant measurement devices, such as the penile plethysmograph, and by careful observation of sexual activity in the laboratory, they were able to document and describe human sexual response. It was through their work that we first knew what happens in female sexual arousal, and they proved that stimulation leading to orgasm could result from both clitoral and vaginal sources. Their study proved women could be multiorgasmic within one sexual activity cycle. Masters and Johnson also did extensive studies on sexuality and the aging process, on homosexual interaction, and on sexual dysfunction.

Based on their research, the team described the four stages of the human sexual-response cycle: excitement, plateau, orgasm, and resolution. Their articulation of the response has held up over the years, even though some of their specific findings have been shown to have a cultural bias.

Human sexuality pioneers and partners William Masters and Virginia Johnson, c. late 1970s. The two were also married from 1971 to 1993.

SEE ALSO *Psychopathia Sexualis* (1886), Sex Roles (1944)

MARTIN LUTHER KING JR., PSYCHOLOGY, AND SOCIAL JUSTICE

Martin Luther King Jr. (1929–68)

IN SEPTEMBER OF 1967, less than a year before he was assassinated, Martin Luther King Jr. gave an electrifying address to more than five thousand members of the American Psychological Association (APA) in Washington, D.C. The presence of King at APA was unprecedented; in fact, race and social problems were not issues that the leadership of APA had ever addressed effectively.

The organized discipline of psychology in the United States was largely conservative in its view of the need to make their science and practice relevant to social problems, despite the saliency of the long civil rights struggle in the United States. But a group affiliated with APA, the Society for the Psychological Study of Social Issues (SPSSI), invited King to give an address at the annual APA convention. King spoke on "The Role of the Behavioral Scientist in the Civil Rights Movement." The speech galvanized many psychologists and led them to become more involved in social issues. The very next year, APA approached Kenneth B. Clark, a prominent African American social psychologist and friend of King's, to run for the APA presidency. He was the only African American to be president of APA until the appointment of Jessica Henderson Daniel in 2018 and Rosie Phillips Davis in 2019.

Prior to this time, Clark had not been actively involved in APA. The research on racial identity conducted by Clark and his wife, Mamie Phipps Clark, known as the Doll Studies, was cited in the Supreme Court's 1954 decision in *Brown v. Board of Education of Topeka*. This had made him a public figure, with influence far beyond the field of social psychology. Since then, Clark had grown pessimistic about the possibility of a just society that was free from racism. He wrote a friend, "How long can our nation continue the tremendous wastage of human intellectual resources demanded by racism?"

King's speech made a difference. By the 1970s, there were active efforts to create more opportunities for graduate training in psychology to students of color.

> [King's] speech galvanized many psychologists and led them to become more involved in social issues.

SEE ALSO The Doll Studies: Racism and Child Self-Image (1943), Black Psychology (1970), The BITCH Test (1970), Liberation Psychology (1989)

ATTACHMENT THEORY

John Bowlby (1907–90)

BY THE END OF WORLD WAR II, thousands of infants and young children had been separated from their parents during the bombing of London and other English cities, with grave psychological consequences. In 1946, John Bowlby, a young psychiatrist who studied how children's experiences within their families influenced personality development, became the head of London's Tavistock Clinic Department for Children and Families. Bowlby became dissatisfied with psychoanalytic theories about children's anxieties related to separation. At this time, he became acquainted with the work of ethologists Niko Tinbergen and Konrad Lorenz, who studied parent-offspring behavior in a variety of species.

> Bowlby theorized that infant attachment to its caregiver served the evolutionarily adaptive function of protection.

The comparative approach gave Bowlby a new framework with which to study a child's ties to its primary caregiver. By using an ethological framework, Bowlby theorized that infant attachment to its caregiver served the evolutionarily adaptive function of protection, thus enhancing the likelihood of the child's survival. The early formulations of the theory were tested in research by Bowlby and his colleagues. The research conducted by developmental psychologist Mary Ainsworth proved most important, as she developed an extensive body of findings that established our current typology of secure, avoidant, ambivalent, and disorganized attachment.

Bowlby and others extended the theory to encompass adolescents and adults. While numerous articles were published by Bowlby and others in the 1950s and 1960s, Bowlby published a fully developed theory of attachment in his 1969 book, *Attachment and Loss*. The work now rests on an impressive research foundation that has done much to elaborate our understanding of human development and the clinical implications when it goes awry. Briefly, the theory holds that safety and protection are the core of attachment. Once a child knows it is secure, then it is possible to explore the immediate environment. Once interiorized, such security creates optimal conditions for cognitive, social, emotional, and personality development over the life course. While Bowlby suggested that this model of attachment is universal to the human experience, recent research suggests that there are important cultural variations.

SEE ALSO Bees Dancing, Egg-Rolling Birds, and the New Science of Ethology (1952), Mother Love (1958)

FIVE STAGES OF GRIEF

Elisabeth Kübler-Ross (1926–2004)

A statue of a grieving woman on the tomb of philanthropist William J. Mullen, in Laurel Hill Cemetery, Philadelphia; photograph by Daniel Kornbau.

WHEN WE FACE IMPENDING DEATH or experience the death of someone close to us, we must find a way to deal with our experience. It was the genius of psychiatrist Elisabeth Kübler-Ross to articulate an easily understandable model of five stages of grief—denial, anger, bargaining, depression, and acceptance—in her book *On Death and Dying* (1969).

Denial, the first stage, may occur when we are first told of a life-threatening illness or hear of the death of someone we love. Such denial can be a useful coping mechanism that gives us time to adjust to the news. We soon realize that denial is not enough, and anger may become the dominant emotion. Why me? Why did my friend die? It, too, is a temporary coping mechanism.

The realization that denial and anger will not change reality may lead to bargaining. This may be concomitant with a renewed faith in a higher power, whom we now try to persuade through prayer or pleading to allow our loved one to live a little longer or to give us a few more years of strength.

Once we accept the reality of death, then a great sadness may set in. And with it may come a period of depression and passivity, in which we refuse to engage the world in the usual way.

Finally, we come to acceptance. In this stage we accept the reality of our loss or impending loss. With this acceptance may come peace and a new engagement with the world.

Kübler-Ross initially proposed the model in relation to death. But over time it has proven useful as a way to understand any major loss, such as divorce or loss of a job. Although the general public has found the model of great utility, the scientific community finds it lacking in scientific rigor.

SEE ALSO *The Interpretation of Dreams* Inaugurates the Century of Psychology (1900), Logotherapy and the Search for Meaning (1946)

BLACK PSYCHOLOGY

Joseph L. White (1928–2017), Robert V. Guthrie (1930–2005)

AFRICAN AMERICAN PSYCHOLOGIST Dr. Joseph L. White coined the term *Black psychology* in his 1970 article for *Ebony* magazine titled "Toward a Black Psychology." The term described a new direction in American psychology led by African American psychologists, who had only recently formed the Association of Black Psychologists (ABPsi) in 1968. American psychology at this time had a long history of discriminatory theories and practices, typically emphasizing perceived deficits of Black families, Black children, and Black individuals, while ignoring the social and class structures that provided whites with more supportive, intellectually rich environments and educational opportunities. Intelligence tests were used to maintain the supposed superior intelligence of whites.

In his seminal book *Even the Rat Was White: A Historical View of Psychology* (1976), African American psychologist Robert Guthrie documented the underrepresentation of blacks, Latinos, Asians, and American Indians in the field of psychology. In the 1960s, the emergent black nationalist movement and the work of such figures as Malcolm X, Stokely Carmichael, H. Rap Brown, and others made terms and phrases such as Black Power, Black Pride, and Black Is Beautiful commonplace in African American communities, indicating a new consciousness of pride and achievement. Influenced by this movement, a handful of young African American psychologists created Black psychology, grounded in the positive values of the African American community, such as resilience and social support. Black psychology was more than a reaction to oppression; its focus was on the strengths and spirit of African Americans.

The impact of Black psychology on theory, research, and practice in American psychology has been profound, and it continues to the present.

For example, theories of Black identity have enriched the psychological study of identity formation, and African American psychologists have articulated effective approaches to psychotherapy that draw on the Black experience in America.

Joseph L. White speaking in 2014 at the UC Irvine Cross-Cultural Center, where he was professor emeritus of the School of Social Science.

SEE ALSO Army Intelligence Tests and Scientific Racism (1921), Martin Luther King Jr., Psychology, and Social Justice (1967), The BITCH Test (1970), Resilience (1973)

THE BITCH TEST

Robert L. Williams (1930–2020)

BY THE 1960S, the number of psychologists of color in the United States was finally on the increase after decades of resistance by the psychological establishment. Once in, they encountered a particularly hostile discipline. In particular there was a tradition of using psychological tests, especially intelligence tests, to maintain racial oppression and inequality.

The formation of the Association of Black Psychologists (ABPsi) in 1968 had given voice to the concerns of African American psychologists about the use of tests in support of discriminatory policies. The work of ABPsi drew upon their contemporary experience as well as on the work of African American and Chicano psychologists of the 1920s and 1930s, such as Herman Canady, Albert Beckham, and George Sanchez. These psychologists and their colleagues had skillfully debunked the claims of racial superiority based on intelligence test results.

The attitude in the late 1960s was more militant. Robert Williams, cofounder and second president of ABPsi, had experienced the negative consequences of biased psychological testing. He began a project to construct a culturally specific test, the Black Intelligence Test of Cultural Homogeneity (BITCH), published in 1970. As Williams wrote at the time, "A 'culture specific' test is used to determine the taker's ability to function symbolically or to think in terms of his own culture and environment." The test was intended to determine the impact of cultural influence on test taking. The BITCH results captured a greater range of intellectual ability in Black children than the standard intelligence tests then in use. Williams and his colleagues, especially African American psychologist Harold Dent, further pursued the question of biased testing.

By the late 1970s, the court of appeals ruled in the case of *Larry P. v. Riles* that intelligence tests could not be used to track racial or ethnic minority children into classes for the mentally retarded.

Dr. Robert L. Williams, left, and Dr. Michael Connor, right, c. 2009. Dr. Williams was one of the founders of the Association of Black Psychology, the developer of the BITCH test, and the creator of Ebonics.

SEE ALSO Army Intelligence Tests and Scientific Racism (1921), Black Psychology (1970)

STANFORD PRISON EXPERIMENT

Philip G. Zimbardo (b. 1933)

A LONG-RUNNING DEBATE in American social psychology has been whether we should attribute more importance to the person or the situation in regard to behavior. An experiment conducted by Stanford University psychologist Phil Zimbardo came down decidedly on the power of the situation.

> The "prisoners" and the "guards" were all part of an experiment to investigate the power of the situation in shaping our behavior.

In the summer of 1971, police picked up ten Stanford University students who had volunteered to participate in a psychological experiment. It was a simulated arrest, but that was not immediately clear to the volunteers. They were handcuffed, fingerprinted, and left in solitary cells. The warden announced the rules of the prison, including the threat of further punishment if they broke the rules. The warden then turned the prisoners over to the guards. The "prisoners" and the "guards" were all part of an experiment to investigate the power of the situation in shaping our behavior.

The "prison" was in the basement of Stanford's Psychology Department; thus there were no windows, and no way to tell whether it was day or night. It quickly became a very stressful experience for the prisoners; the guards denied them bathroom visits, woke them after only a brief period of sleep, yelled at them, and generally sought to dehumanize them.

Five of the prisoners broke down and had to be released; others became blindly obedient to the authority of the guards and turned on their fellow prisoners in order to obtain favors from the guards. The guards took on their roles with a vengeance and became abusive. Zimbardo also identified with his role as superintendent and, as he later acknowledged, lost sight of the event as an experiment, overlooking the suffering he was causing the student-prisoners. After five days, Zimbardo stopped the project and apologized for allowing the situation to get out of hand.

Zimbardo revisited the implications of the prison experiment when the abuses at Iraq's Abu Ghraib prison came to light in 2004. His best-selling book *The Lucifer Effect: Understanding How Good People Turn Evil* (2007) reexamined the person-situation debate and concluded that both the Stanford prison experiment and Abu Ghraib are chilling reminders of what everyday people are capable of doing in response to stressful situations.

SEE ALSO Conformity and Independence (1951), Milgram's Obedience Experiments (1963), Social Identity Theory (1979)

RESILIENCE

Norman Garmezy (1918–2009)

THE WORD *RESILIENCE* ORIGINATED in engineering and materials science and referred to the ability of a material to return to its original shape or position after stress. Resilience, in its contemporary sense of the ability to successfully cope with difficulties, dates from the late 1960s.

In the 1960s, two apparently diverse streams in American life came together that led to a recognition of the importance of resilience. One stream was the new research that linked behavior and lifestyle factors to a variety of health outcomes, such as smoking and lung cancer. The other stream was the heightened awareness of social problems, especially racism, and their incredibly high cost in terms of public and personal health.

The work of Norman Garmezy in the late 1960s brought these streams together. His study of children vulnerable to schizophrenia (for example, those who were poor or had a schizophrenic parent) revealed that many of these children never developed the disease. Garmezy was especially concerned about children who were otherwise disadvantaged, such as African American children in large cities. The studies on these children, which he published in 1973, launched the contemporary examination of psychological resilience. At almost the same time, a new cohort of African American psychologists was writing about the strengths, including resilience, of Black families and communities.

Since that time, research has uncovered many of the factors that characterize resilience. One researcher has called resilience "ordinary magic"—that is, the factors that lead to resilience are all facets of what human beings have evolved to do in order to adapt to a sometimes hostile and threatening environment. Good interpersonal skills, self-confidence, and positive caregiving are among these protective factors. More recently, cultural factors have also been shown to be important in the experience of resilience.

Just as some plants and animals can thrive under difficult conditions, so can humans, as three generations of psychological research has now shown.

SEE ALSO The Discovery of Stress (1950), Black Psychology (1970)

JUDGMENT UNDER UNCERTAINTY: HUMAN RATIONALITY

Daniel Kahneman (b. 1934), Amos Tversky (1937–96)

A FRIEND SUGGESTS THAT YOU GO on a blind date with a person whom he describes as very attractive, quiet, and thoughtful. How do you make the judgment whether you want to go out with this person? Cognitive psychologists suggest that you are likely to use one of several heuristics, or mental shortcuts, to help you decide.

In an article published in *Science* in 1974 titled "Judgment Under Uncertainty: Heuristics and Biases," psychologists Daniel Kahneman and Amos Tversky analyzed how we use heuristics to help us make decisions. As a result of their work, we now better understand the reasons we often make mistakes in our judgment. By extension, they have shown that humans are not necessarily the rational creatures that science supposes.

In the article and in subsequent publications, Kahneman and Tversky showed how humans are very susceptible to erroneous intuitions, regardless of intelligence. Their article opened up a

> Kahneman and Tversky showed how humans are very susceptible to erroneous intuitions, regardless of intelligence.

new domain of research in philosophy, psychology, and cognitive science. Kahneman and Tversky then turned to the study of decision making, which led to their development of prospect theory, which proposes that humans use heuristics to make decisions based on the possible value of losses and gains and not on the final outcome. The theory helped spawn the modern field of behavioral economics and led to Kahneman receiving the Nobel Prize in economics in 2002 (Tversky had died in 1996, and the Nobel is not awarded posthumously).

Here is an example of one such heuristic. We may wonder if taking the surface streets to work during rush hour is faster than taking the expressway. We recall our own experiences of driving to work to determine which strategy works best. If the thought of arriving sooner at work by taking surface streets comes to mind more easily, then our judgment may be that doing so is the best strategy. This is the availability heuristic. But judging by ease of recall may not be a consistently good strategy, as the expressway may frequently be faster in reality.

SEE ALSO Cognitive Therapy (1955), Cognitive Dissonance: How Humans Maintain Psychological Consistency (1957)

1975

SIKOLOHIYANG PILIPINO

Alfredo Lagmay (1919–2005),
Virgilio Enriquez (1942–94)

THE PHILIPPINES WAS RULED BY SPAIN for three centuries; then from 1898 until 1946, the country was governed by the United States. After the country's release from American sovereignty, many Filipinos sought to create institutions and approaches that reflected purely Filipino beliefs and values. Alfredo Lagmay and Virgilio Enriquez led this effort in psychology. After Lagmay became the chair of the psychology department at the University of the Philippines in Manila, Enriquez returned to the Philippines from the United States, where he had received his doctoral degree. Together the two men created Sikolohiyang Pilipino ("Filipino Psychology"), which is intended to decolonize the Filipino psyche after the long period of Western domination. The formal beginnings of this movement were established at the first National Conference on Filipino Psychology, held in 1975 and chaired by Enriquez.

Lagmay and Enriquez founded the Philippine Psychology Research and Training House, where hundreds of students engaged in developing Sikolohiyang Pilipino. The development of research methods that accord with Filipino culture is one of the most singular innovations of Sikolohiyang Pilipino. Enriquez established the technique of "groping" toward an appropriate design and methodology as the project moved forward, rather than beginning with a strategy and shaping the questions to fit the methods a priori.

Rooted in Filipino culture and history, Sikolohiyang Pilipino emphasizes that psychological knowledge arises from the collaborative demands of relationships and not strictly from an individual psychological development. One must see the participant as another human being, not as a data point,

and begin to build trust and genuineness before proceeding with
data collection.

Enriquez and Lagmay insisted
that Filipino values must be at the
center of Sikolohiyang Pilipino.
Thus the study of a sense of propriety (hiya), gratitude and solidarity (utang na loob), and, most
important, shared identity (kapwa)
assumed prominence. Kapwa, for
instance, leads us to treat others
as fellow human beings, worthy
of respect; whether that person

Sikolohiyang Pilipino emphasizes that psychological knowledge arises from the collaborative demands of relationships.

is an insider or outsider determines the kind and level of interaction.
Sikolohiyang Pilipino remains a vibrant force in the Philippines today.

SEE ALSO Confucian Psychology (c. 500 BCE), Culture Determines What Counts
as Mental Illness (1904), Cultural Relativism: Culture, Sex, and Coming of Age
(1928)

PSYCHONEUROIMMUNOLOGY

Robert Ader (1932–2011), Candace B. Pert (1946–2013)

THE IMMUNE SYSTEM FUNCTIONS as a surveillance and defense network within the body. It protects against infections and other "foreign" invaders, but it has also been implicated in autoimmune disorders, such as arthritis. Psychoneuroimmunology (PNI) is an approach that studies the interactions of the immune system, neuroendocrine processes, and psychological factors in order to understand health and disease.

The fact that psychological factors can affect the immune system is a relatively recent discovery, made by psychologist Robert Ader in 1975. It was first observed in rats that learned to avoid sweetened water when it was paired with a nausea-inducing drug that also suppressed the immune system. Ader's team then found that the sweetened water alone would suppress immune function, indicating that psychological processes such as learning are linked to the immune system.

About ten years later, neuroscientist and pharmacologist Candace Pert discovered that neurotransmitters have direct interactions with the immune system; further research indicated that there are intricate linkages between emotional states and immune function. This work suggests a potentially important connection between clinical anxiety, major depression, and physical health.

Broadly, research has shown that many stressors, from daily hassles like finding parking to major natural disasters, can have a negative effect on immunocompetence, or the capability for a normal immune response. The larger question is whether the psychological impact of stressors on the immune system can make a difference in terms of health. There is now a large body of research that shows that people under stress are more vulnerable to infectious diseases, ranging from colds and flu to chicken pox and

Covid-19. Chronic diseases, such as coronary heart disease, can be exacerbated by stress-related changes in immune system functions. Depression, in particular, appears to have the potential to significantly lower immunocompetence. PNI has emerged as one of the twenty-first century's clearest examples of a true mind-body connection.

Since the 1970s, research has uncovered the close interworking of psychological and biological factors, including our immune system, in keeping us healthy. Depression has the potential to significantly lower immunocompetence.

SEE ALSO The Discovery of Stress (1950), Resilience (1973), Mindfulness and Mind-Body Medicine (1993)

THEORY OF MIND

David Premack (b. 1925)

THE ABILITY TO IMAGINE what other people feel or think and to respond accordingly is one of the most important accomplishments of social development. Modern developmental science has been intensively studying this ability in infants, children, chimpanzees, and even rodents for about thirty years.

Developmental psychologists call this ability theory of mind (ToM). It is a principle that can be found in several of the world's major religions; but in psychology, David Premack and Guy Woodruff offered one of the first full expressions of ToM in 1978. Formally, theory of mind refers to children's understanding that others also have thoughts, beliefs, objectives, and emotions. Without ToM, the child would not be able to pick up on the social cues or intentions of others, as is often the case when a child suffers from autism.

> Theory of mind refers to children's understanding that others also have thoughts, beliefs, objectives, and emotions.

Theory of mind is a developmental process that, in normally developing children, is usually fully in place by about age four or five. Scientists have found that the critical precursors of ToM occur as early as seven to nine months as the infant learns that the attention of others can be directed by simple tasks like pointing or reaching. By the end of the first year, infants are beginning to understand that people have intentions. But it is not until about age four or five that children truly understand that there is a link between how others feel or think and what they do.

Neuroscientists using brain-imaging techniques have shown that this is exactly the age when the prefrontal cortex of the brain is rapidly maturing. For children with autism, this is not the case, although there are interventions that can help improve the brain's responses in children with autism.

Theory of mind is crucially important for displaying empathy and caring for others. It makes it possible for us to be socially competent. Research on ToM has greatly facilitated our understanding of children's social development, with implications for emotional and cognitive development. It is also a principle that facilitated the reception of mirror neurons.

SEE ALSO Can Apes Learn Human Language? (1909), Mirror Neurons (1992)

ECOLOGICAL SYSTEMS THEORY

Urie Bronfenbrenner (1917–2005)

AMERICAN DEVELOPMENTAL PSYCHOLOGY was once characterized as "the science of the strange behavior of children in strange situations with strange adults for the briefest possible periods of time." The person who made that statement—Urie Bronfenbrenner—also offered an alternative to such an unnaturalistic approach.

One of the preeminent American psychologists of the twentieth century, Bronfenbrenner was born in Russia and "developed" in the United States. By the late 1960s, he was chafing at the narrow, artificial approach that then characterized American developmental psychology. To create what he called the ecology of the child, he borrowed from systems theory, which posits that to study any phenomenon, one must consider it in relation to its broader contexts. His fully articulated theory was published in 1979 as *The Ecology of Human Development*.

Bronfenbrenner proposed that human development occurs within four nested systems and that each must be considered both alone and in relation to one other. The microsystem is the child's personal environment, made up of parents, peers, and the institutions that the child directly interacts with. The mesosystem is the system of interactions among the various components of the microsystem, such as parents and teachers, parents and the child's peers, or the family and religious institutions.

The next level of complexity is the exosystem; these are the contexts that affect development but with which the child does not directly interact. An example would be the work situations of the parents, which could have an influence on the child in terms of day care, or the fact of having a parent who travels a lot for work. Finally, the macrosystem is the larger cultural or national situation that the child lives within, such as the level of governmental support for higher education, which could shape the child's choices.

The ecological model has provided a rich metaperspective on human development. It has made it possible to think broadly about the complexity and richness of the ways in which our lives are shaped.

Bronfenbrenner proposed that human development occurs within four nested systems.

SEE ALSO Zone of Proximal Development (1934), Head Start (1965)

SOCIAL IDENTITY THEORY

Henri Tajfel (1919–82)

IS PREJUDICE PRIMARILY due to personality factors, or do group membership and collective identity play the most prominent roles? Social psychologist Henri Tajfel argued for the importance of group membership in generating prejudice. Tajfel was born in Poland to Jewish parents, but left Poland to study in Paris for his graduate degree. He was there when World War II began, so he enlisted in the French army. He was captured and spent the remainder of the war in Nazi concentration camps. When the war was over, he discovered that his entire family had been killed by the Nazis. These experiences led to his research program on intergroup behavior and how prejudice forms.

Tajfel found that merely classifying people into one group or another led to bias.

Based on his wartime experience, Tajfel believed that prejudice and hatred are influenced by the groups we belong to. His early research on categorization showed that grouping objects into categories labeled A and B led to false judgments of similarity within each group and an exaggeration of difference between the groups. Building on this research, Tajfel found that merely classifying people into one group or another led to bias. Participants began to assert the superiority of their own group and to diminish the other group. He and his student John Turner published a full theory of social identity in 1979 in a book chapter entitled

"An Integrative Theory of Intergroup Conflict." After Tajfel's death in 1982, Turner added new material from Tajfel's research and published it in 1986 as "The Social Identity Theory of Intergroup Relations."

Tajfel used his research results to argue that we derive our social identity from group membership, and we then use group membership to enhance a positive view of ourselves. One way we do this is to join groups that give us a positive identity; another way is to claim that the groups to which we belong are the best. To further bolster our positive self-view, we tend to overstate how different our group is from another. Group membership has a positive effect on our self-view, but it may also lead us to discriminate and form prejudices against members of other groups.

SEE ALSO Conformity and Independence (1951), Contact Hypothesis or How to Reduce Racism and Bias (1954)

NURTURANT-TASK
MODEL OF LEADERSHIP

Jai B. P. Sinha (b. 1936)

A LONG TRADITION OF LEADERSHIP studies in Western psychology appeared to establish the superiority and attractiveness of democratic leadership styles. Yet as the scientific discipline of psychology spread across the world after World War II, dissent about this and other matters appeared. In many countries, efforts began to develop a psychology that reflected local culture and intellectual traditions, such as Sikolohiyang Pilipino in the Philippines.

In India, Jai B. P. Sinha developed an organizational leadership model that was based in Indian familial and social relations; the first full explication of his model was published was published in 1979 as *The Nurturant-Task Leader* in the *ASCI Journal of Management*. Sinha earned his doctorate at Ohio State University, where he was immersed in the best American tradition of social psychology.

Once back in India, Sinha established himself as an important figure in Indian psychology. He soon realized that the cultural traditions of India provided a better foundation for a nuanced and subtle psychology—the kind best suited for understanding the Indian work environment—than imported Western psychology. Sinha posited that, in India, meaningfulness is inextricably linked to relationships with others and that the goal of life is to find harmony with both nature and society. This is the foundation of the relationship between manager (or leader) and employee as well.

Beginning in the 1970s, Sinha focused on the study of leadership and its role in Indian business. Sinha and his research group showed that Indians respond best to what they called the nurturant-task model of leadership, in which the manager or leader provides high expectations of productivity combined with a nurturing relationship with the worker. In doing so, the leader facilitates the development of the subordinate toward greater self-motivation and less dependence on the leader. Sinha argued that this management style reflects the dependency patterns of Indian culture, the tendency to personalize relationships, and status consciousness, and he showed how using this style could result in greater productivity on the part of the Indian workforce.

[In] the nurturant-task model of leadership .... the manager or leader provides high expectations of productivity combined with a nurturing relationship with the worker.

SEE ALSO Transforming Western Psychology in India (1915), Cultural Relativism: Culture, Sex, and Coming of Age (1928), Sikolohiyang Pilipino (1975)

POST-TRAUMATIC
STRESS DISORDER (PTSD)

"THE CATASTROPHIC STRESS OF COMBAT leaves its marks on the psyche that require both time and confrontation to erase." These words written in the context of returning Vietnam War veterans apply equally well to soldiers of earlier wars. During World War II, hundreds of thousands of young American soldiers experienced what was then called war neurosis or combat fatigue. In World War I, thousands of soldiers on both sides experienced severe psychological distress in what was labeled shell shock. The problems of Vietnam veterans seemed more severe and endured for years after they returned home. Higher rates of drug abuse, spousal abuse, divorce, and suicide were reported than in the aftermath of earlier wars.

Unfortunately, at the time when the Vietnam War ended, many mental health professionals refused to recognize that the problems of war veterans often persisted after the war. In the diagnostic manual of American psychiatry, there was no term specific to the symptoms of those who had undergone traumatic experiences, whether of war or natural disasters. Yet it was clear that thousands of the Vietnam veterans were suffering and causing real damage to their families and to the social fabric. By the late 1970s, veterans joined cause with survivors of the Nazi Holocaust and other disasters and atrocities to convince the mental health professions of a need for a new diagnostic category that could lead to research and effective interventions: Post-Traumatic Stress Disorder appeared for the first time in *DSM-III* in 1980.

Since then, trauma and its effects have been recognized in many situations, including child abuse, domestic violence, rape, terrorism, and many other experiences. Models of coping, adaptation, and resilience, along with a variety of treatments, have evolved to meet the rising incidence of PTSD.

PFC D. R. Howe treats the wounds of PFC D. A. Crum during 1st Marine Division operations in the Tet Offensive at Hue, February 1968. PTSD came into usage as a term to describe the psychological effect of combat in Vietnam on many US soldiers.

SEE ALSO: The Discovery of Stress (1950), Resilience (1973), Positive Psychology (2000)

IN A DIFFERENT VOICE:
WOMEN AND MORAL DEVELOPMENT

Carol Gilligan (b. 1936)

HOW DO PEOPLE RESOLVE real-life moral dilemmas? This was the question that intrigued Carol Gilligan when she came to Harvard as an instructor of psychology in the late 1960s. Her interest was sparked by psychologist Lawrence Kohlberg's research on moral development. Kohlberg's work had shown that women do not generally exhibit the highest level of moral reasoning, termed "justice-oriented reasoning," as often as men. But Gilligan wanted to take her research in a different direction. Whereas Kohlberg's participants had responded to hypothetical moral dilemmas, Gilligan decided to interview participants facing the real-life dilemma of whether or not to terminate a pregnancy.

In the course of conducting her research, she had a startling insight: the reason women scored lower in Kohlberg's scheme was because it was based entirely on results from male participants, yet it was taken to represent a universal standard. By including only men in his studies, he had missed other styles and forms of reasoning. Gilligan described the style of reasoning she heard in her participants' accounts as an "ethic of care"; that is, women repeatedly told her that their decisions about whether or not to have an abortion were based on the value of remaining in a relationship and not inflicting pain on others.

She wrote up her study and her conclusions in the landmark book *In a Different Voice: A Psychological Theory of Women's Development*, published in 1982. In it she argued that women's moral decision-making processes did not map well onto prevailing psychological theories constructed within an all-male framework. She outlined the ethic of care and suggested that although it was more commonly used by women, we should seek to make it a more prominent part of all human development. Her work continues to influence the debate about gender differences, but, perhaps more important, it exposed the deeply androcentric basis of much of psychological theory up to that time.

Carol Gilligan argued that women's moral decision-making processes did not map well onto prevailing psychological theories constructed within an all-male framework, and initiated what is now a major project to articulate important gender differences in development, especially around moral issues.

SEE ALSO Variability Hypothesis: Gender and Genius (1914), Friedan's *The Feminine Mystique* (1963)

MULTIPLE INTELLIGENCES

Howard E. Gardner (b. 1943)

ONE OF THE OLDEST ARGUMENTS in modern psychology is whether intelligence is a single ability, commonly known as g or the g *factor*, or is better understood as a group of several distinct cognitive abilities. In the United States, the single-ability view was dominant for most of the twentieth century. But in the seminal publication *Frames of Mind: The Theory of Multiple Intelligences* (1983), psychologist Howard Gardner changed the conversation about the nature of intelligence.

Gardner has noted that it was his training in the arts that led him to reconsider the notion of a single intellectual ability. He became involved with Project Zero, a program at Harvard's Graduate School of Education that sought to improve education in the arts and promote it as a method of learning about and knowing the world. Later work on brain functioning in people suffering from a brain injury helped him link cognitive development, the arts, and how the brain works.

From this association he proposed that there are eight identified intelligences: linguistic intelligence, logical-mathematical intelligence, spatial intelligence, musical intelligence, bodily-kinesthetic intelligence, naturalistic intelligence, interpersonal intelligence, and intrapersonal intelligence. Each has its own neurological brain network, as evidenced by the fact that a person can suffer an injury and lose one kind of intelligence while the others are fully functioning.

Culture also plays an important role in the expression of our intelligences. In some societies, such as in sub-Saharan Africa, social understanding is highly valued, and a person who displays a high degree of social understanding is considered very intelligent. In Western societies, linguistic intelligence is highly valued, and a person will be considered very smart if he or she displays high-level language skills.

Gardner's theory has been highly influential in changing how American educators think about the educational needs of children. Because of his successful challenge of the traditional theory of a single intelligence, the door was opened to other models of intelligence, such as emotional intelligence, which author and science journalist Daniel Goleman explored in his 1995 best-selling book *Emotional Intelligence: Why It Can Matter More than IQ*.

> Each [intelligence] has its own neurological brain network . . . . Culture also plays an important role in the expression of our intelligences.

SEE ALSO Social Ontogenesis: Culture and Development in Africa (1992)

LIBERATION PSYCHOLOGY

Paulo Freire (1921–97),
Ignacio Martín-Baró (1942–89)

IN THE MID-TWENTIETH CENTURY in Latin America, popular protests against poverty and the lack of attention to the needs of the poor and marginalized gave rise within the Roman Catholic Church to a movement called liberation theology. Running parallel with theological developments at the time, liberation psychology emphasized the use of social science to achieve community action and justice. Of the many psychologists involved, none was more important than the Jesuit psychologist Ignacio Martín-Baró. He argued that true knowledge is concerned with transforming the conditions of the oppressed. This kind of psychological knowledge, he said, was a force for liberation.

> Liberation psychology emphasized the use of social science to achieve community action and justice.

Martín-Baró drew on the earlier work of Brazilian Paulo Freire and his concept of conscientization, or gaining a critical consciousness about how political structures can oppress the human mind. Recognition of this oppression can lead to personal psychological growth and efforts to make a more just society, which opens up new ideas for what is possible, not just personally but for civilization. Because the government perceived his work as threatening to their regime, Martín-Baró was assassinated along with six of his Jesuit brothers by a US-trained Salvadoran death squad in 1989.

His work continues and now is an important theoretical and practical force around the world.

Following Martín-Baró, contemporary liberation psychology seeks to serve the needs of everyday people. The power of Martín-Baró's ideas and practices is clear from the fact that he was assassinated. In his view, psychology, in theory and practice, must be oriented toward the deep social problems of Latin America. In one of his essays, translated into English after his death, he wrote:

> If as psychologists we wish to make a contribution to the social development of Latin America, we have to redesign our theoretical and practical tools from the standpoint of the lives of our own people, from their sufferings, aspirations, and struggles. We must affirm that any effort at developing a psychology that will contribute to the liberation of our peoples has to mean the creation of a liberation psychology.

SEE ALSO Black Psychology (1970), Sikolohiyang Pilipino (1975)

FLOW:
THE EXPERIENCE
OF OPTIMAL LIVING

Mihaly Csikszentmihalyi (b. 1934)

WHAT MIGHT BEING COMPLETELY ABSORBED in gardening and being "in the zone" while playing basketball have in common? They may both indicate that an individual is experiencing flow, a state of being so at one with the moment that a person is said to be living optimally. Flow is, according to Hungarian American psychologist Mihaly Csikszentmihalyi, who identified the phenomenon, the hallmark of what it means to have a good life. Like Abraham Maslow's "peak experience," flow is an experience of full engagement with the moment one is in.

The research that led to the concept of flow began in the 1960s, when Csikszentmihalyi was studying the creative process in visual artists. He noticed that artists often painted with a single-minded persistence that seemed to defy fatigue and hunger. Yet when the painting was complete, the artists often had little interest in it. It was as though the act of being absorbed in the painting was the reward. Csikszentmihalyi then set out to systematically study this hypothesis. He found that the experience could occur during almost any activity in almost any field, such as the arts, sports, or medicine.

Csikszentmihalyi's research indicated two conditions that make flow likely. The first is that the activity must stretch a person's skill level; that is, a person must experience the activity as a just-manageable challenge. Second, there must be opportunities for continuous feedback that allow for constant adjustment as the activity proceeds. Once these conditions are met, a person experiences a subjective state marked by a focused concentration that merges awareness and action. Time seems to pass quickly, because the person seems to forget about himself or herself as an entity separate from the activity. When in flow, a person finds the activity itself intensely rewarding, apart from the immediate result.

There have been attempts to structure environments to enhance the likelihood of the flow experience. The Key School in Indianapolis created the Flow Activities Center, where schoolchildren can pursue activities that interest them without teachers or other adults imposing demands on them. One study of the center indicated that the children who participated reported increases in intrinsic motivation regarding their education. There are now numerous sites where flow principles have been introduced, including the Getty Museum in Los Angeles, a Nissan assembly plant, and a psychotherapy practice in Milan, Italy.

> Time seems to pass quickly, because the person seems to forget about himself or herself as an entity separate from the activity.

SEE ALSO Maslow Creates the Hierarchy of Needs (1943), Humanistic Psychology (1961), Positive Psychology (2000)

MIRROR NEURONS

Giacomo Rizzolatti (b. 1937)

MONKEY SEE, MONKEY DO? It turns out that monkeys, humans, birds, and other species have specialized brain cells that are exquisitely sensitive to the actions of others. These brain cells are called mirror neurons, and they represent an exciting new field of psychological science for the twenty-first century. Mirror neurons were first discovered by neuroscientist Giacomo

Mirror neurons fire when an animal or person observes another animal or person performing an action; it is also thought that the intensity of mirror neuron activation is related to the motor skills of the observer. If you are a skilled tennis player, then your mirror neurons fire more intensely when you are watching an ace player than they would in the brain of someone less proficient.

Rizzolatti and his colleagues at the University of Padua. Their first attempts to publish their findings were rejected because the journal they submitted to thought the subject would not be of interest to other scientists! (The paper was eventually published in 1992.)

What Rizzolatti found was that these neurons fire (or become active) when an animal or person observes another animal or person, even a member of a different species, performing an action. This is how they got their name: they mirror the actions of other neurons and fire as if they were performing the action themselves. For example, when we see another person reaching for a cookie, our brains act as though we are reaching for a cookie. This indicates that there are direct brain links between our perceptions and our actions.

In humans, it is thought that the mirror system develops in the first year of life and has links with infant imitation and interaction with caregivers. There are many nuances about mirror neurons that have now been discovered. One is that the intensity of mirror neuron activation is related to the motor skills of the observer. So if you are a really good tennis player, then the neurons in the mirror network of your brain fire more intensely when you are watching Roger Federer than they would in the brain of someone who is less skilled at tennis.

Scientists and philosophers are very excited by mirror neurons. It is thought that we now may be able to better understand empathy, autism, language, and the intentions of others through research on these specialized brain cells.

SEE ALSO Theory of Mind (1978)

SOCIAL ONTOGENESIS: CULTURE AND DEVELOPMENT IN AFRICA

A. Bame Nsamenang (b. 1951)

WITH THE NOTABLE EXCEPTION of South Africa, the discipline of psychology was not well established in sub-Saharan Africa until the late twentieth century. Until the work of Professor A. Bame Nsamenang and a few others was brought to light beginning in the 1980s, most African psychology mirrored the individualistic perspective of Westerners. Nsamenang, however, developed a theory of human development grounded in the sociocentric world-view of most African societies. In his book *Human Development in Cultural Context: A Third World Perspective* (1992), Nsamenang argued that African theories of human development place primary emphasis on social ontogenesis; that is, development occurs as the individual participates in the cultural activities of the community.

> An African view of development . . . is relational, requiring a connection to the community.

An African view of development incorporates both metaphysical and experiential phases. The spiritual self begins with conception and ends when a person is given his or her name. The experiential self then takes over and carries a person through to biological death. The final stage is ancestral selfhood, in which the self continues in the memories and rituals of the living. In some cultural expressions, it may be reincarnated.

Experiential selfhood is the domain of social ontogenesis. It comprises seven stages: the newborn, a period of social priming, followed by social apprenticing, then a social entrée, social internment, adulthood, and, finally, death. Each stage has its own developmental tasks framed by the cultural expectations of the community. Development is relational, requiring a connection to the community. In this model, human beings need social responsibility to attain full personhood, and guidance is devoted to helping children become socially responsible.

How is intelligence recognized? As a child develops, he or she is assigned a task that serves the community. Adults and older children monitor how well the child completes the task and thus determine when the child is ready to take on more complex and difficult chores. Intelligence is described in social terms and by a person's level of social responsibility rather than by an abstract score on a test.

By the beginning of the twenty-first century, a robust body of psychological theory, research, and application had been established in sub-Saharan Africa. Much of it focused, as Nsamenang did, on human development and its problems in rapidly changing societies.

SEE ALSO Theory of Mind (1978), Ecological Systems Theory (1979), Multiple Intelligences (1983)

1993

MINDFULNESS AND MIND-BODY MEDICINE

Bill Moyers (b. 1934)

SINCE THE BEGINNINGS of recorded history, people have thought of the mind and body as linked in illness and health. Common examples include traditional Chinese medicine, with its concepts of chi and yin and yang, Ayurvedic and Unani medicine from India, and the temples of Asclepius in ancient Greece. It was only with the writings of the seventeenth-century philosopher René Descartes that the mind and body were separated to obviate potential religious objections to studying the functions of each. Closer to our own time, the Mind-Cure movement in America brought a renewed interest in mind and body relationships.

By the 1990s, the term mind-body medicine began to be used to refer to programmatic research and practice that incorporated a variety of techniques that made the whole person the focus of treatment. While no single individual was responsible for this change of focus, Bill Moyers's 1993 book and television series *Healing and the Mind* presented mind-body medicine in a digestible format to millions of people around the world. Moyers's show and book brought information about stress reduction, meditation, the power of the placebo effect, non-Western healing practices, and other esoteric topics to a mass audience.

The Public Broadcasting Service (PBS) television series had a large viewership, and the accompanying book was a best seller. *Healing and the Mind* became a major influence on the way Americans think about the role of the mind in health and sickness. For example, Moyers introduced Americans to the work of Jon Kabat-Zinn, a molecular biologist and professor at the University of Massachusetts Medical School. Kabat-Zinn founded the

Stress Reduction Clinic at UMass in 1979 and has taught hundreds of medical patients how to use Zen Buddhism–based mindfulness techniques to help them deal with their medical conditions.

Mindfulness techniques have now spread to many domains of health care, including cognitive behavior therapy. Moyers's influence played a major role in stimulating the US Congress to authorize the National Institutes of Health to create the Center for Complementary and Alternative Medicine. Thus, by the end of the twentieth century, psychological factors were officially recognized as playing a critical role in maintaining health and preventing disease.

Healing and the Mind became a major influence on the way Americans think about the role of the mind in health and sickness.

SEE ALSO Buddha's Four Noble Truths (528 BCE), Descartes on Mind and Body (1637), Mind-Cure (1859), The Discovery of Stress (1950), Placebo Effect (1955)

LOOPING EFFECTS OF HUMAN KINDS

Ian Hacking (b. 1936)

HOW DO KINDS OR CATEGORIES of people—such as the homosexual, the multiple personality, and the autistic—come into being? How do classifications of people affect possibilities for action and self-construal by those who become so classified and those who react to them? Canadian philosopher of science Ian Hacking has explored these questions using several examples from the history of the human sciences to demonstrate what he calls the "looping effects of human kinds."

Hacking argues that many kinds of human beings come into existence and are coconstituted with our invention of ways to name them. The homosexual, for example, came into being in the late nineteenth century not because same-sex relationships had not existed before that time but because classifying someone as homosexual or heterosexual became relevant in a way it had not been before then. This in turn creates the possibility of identifying as a certain kind of person. The process whereby people relate to these categories and in turn change the categories is referred to as the looping effect.

In 1995, Hacking published an extended study of this process in *Rewriting the Soul: Multiple Personality and the Sciences of Memory*. In this work, he reconstructs the historically contingent processes that changed the experience of dissociation into the psychiatric category called multiple personality disorder and the effect this new category had on our understanding and behavior.

The looping effects of human kinds has important implications for psychology. Human beings' ability to reflect on their classifications, to change them, and to bring new ways of being into existence means that the very things psychologists study are constantly changing. Since psychologists themselves create new classifications, they are often directly implicated in this process.

A daguerreotype of a gay couple, c. 1850. Ian Hacking posits that new "kinds" of human beings come into being when they are classified; the concept of the homosexual, for example, came into being in the late nineteenth century not because same-sex relationships were a new phenomenon but because classifying someone by their sexual preference became relevant in a new way.

SEE ALSO Sex Roles (1944), Hooker's Research: Homosexuality Is Not an Illness (1957)

STEREOTYPE THREAT

Claude Mason Steele (b. 1946)

WHY DO MANY WOMEN FAIL to perform as well as some men on tests of mathematical ability, even when their histories indicate they are equally capable? Why is the college dropout rate for intelligent and talented African American students so much higher than it is for students of European descent? In 1995, American social psychologist Claude Steele proposed stereotype threat as one possible explanation.

Social psychologists define stereotype threat as a person's fear that he or she will confirm the stereotype of a particular group to which he or she belongs. The presence of this threat indicates that the source of failure or poor performance may lie in the social environment rather than within the individual. Thus the stereotype that men are better at math may depress women's performance on tests of mathematical ability. This is most likely to occur when the stereotype is presented before the test is taken. The negative effect of stereotype threat has been demonstrated in athletics, entrepreneurship, the game of chess, and other domains.

> The source of failure or poor performance may lie in the social environment rather than within the individual.

Steele has focused on the effect of stereotype threat on high-achieving African American students. In the United States, there is a negative stereotype about the intellectual ability of African Americans. In a series of experiments in which a difficult English test was given to bright white and Black students, African Americans did poorly compared to the white students when the test was presented as a test of their verbal abilities (a stereotype threat). When the same test was presented as a study of the ways in which difficult problems are solved and not as a study of intellectual ability (a non-stereotype threat), then there was no difference between the performance of Black students and the performance of white students. Steele found that the way to reduce stereotype threat for African Americans is with explicit information that a test or challenge is racially fair, thus increasing the confidence of Black students by reducing the doubt they might otherwise experience.

SEE ALSO Army Intelligence Tests and Scientific Racism (1921), The Doll Studies: Racism and Child Self-Image (1943), Contact Hypothesis or How to Reduce Racism and Bias (1954)

1996

AUTONOMOUS-RELATIONAL SELF

Çigdem Kagitçibasi (b. 1940)

WESTERN RESEARCHERS TEND TO DICHOTOMIZE cultural notions of self into independent (Western) and collectivist (Eastern) orientations. Thus a child growing up in the United States is expected to be independent and self-reliant, whereas a child growing up in India is likely to have a sense of identity oriented to family relationships. This kind of dichotomizing is, of course, simplistic.

Turkish developmental psychologist Çigdem Kagitçibasi offered a third and more complex approach: the autonomous-relational self. She pointed out that most models of psychological development assume that the goal of development is an autonomous (or independent) adult self. This, Kagitçibasi argued, is predicated on a very Western notion of selfhood. She argued that instead of this model, researchers should place changes in development in a broader cultural context.

Under the pressure of modernization over the last one hundred years, there has been a convergence of independent and collectivist orientations. Globalization has made many Majority World families similar to Western families, but the strength of their cultural traditions has helped them retain close relational ties among their members. This is in contrast to older research, in which autonomy and relatedness were often contrasted as incompatible opposites. Now studies show that autonomy and relatedness are harmonious aspects of the human experience. Along with competence, they make up the three basic human needs found in all societies.

Research from around the world has emphasized the importance of social networks in the maintenance of mental and physical health. Studies conducted among immigrant and refugee populations have been particularly helpful in demonstrating that we as humans are capable of self-governance while being fully dependent on close relationships. For those who migrate from their home to a new culture, the combination of self-sufficiency and close bonds may help a person through the difficulties of adapting to a new society, especially when there are great differences between the receiving culture and the one of origin.

Since Kagitçibasi's articulation of the full-fledged theory in 1996, other investigations have supported the basic approach of the theory of the autonomous-relational self in cultures as diverse as Japan and the Netherlands.

> Studies show that autonomy and relatedness are harmonious aspects of the human experience.

SEE ALSO Culture Determines What Counts as Mental Illness (1904), Cultural Relativism: Culture, Sex, and Coming of Age (1928)

POSITIVE PSYCHOLOGY

Martin E. P. Seligman (b. 1942),
Mihaly Csikszentmihalyi (b. 1934)

IS IT PREFERABLE TO TRY to repair damage or prevent it? Is human life best described in terms of our weaknesses or our strengths? These are important questions for the science of psychology. For much of its existence, American psychology has focused on treatment rather than prevention, and more pages have been devoted to cataloging psychological pathologies than to understanding and promoting human assets. At the beginning of the twenty-first century, that began to change with the advent of positive psychology.

Positive psychology research seeks to catalog human strengths and virtues instead of simply describing human life in terms of our weaknesses or our strengths.

Two psychologists have been at the forefront of positive psychology's development: Martin Seligman and Mihaly Csikszentmihalyi. Seligman's journey began with work on experimental psychopathology—that is, using animal models to understand human mental disorders. He described how organisms can develop learned helplessness. By the early 1990s, he was writing about how optimism can be taught. The Hungarian-born Csikszentmihalyi spent many years studying creativity and optimal experience, or flow. They famously met when Seligman spotted Csikszentmihalyi struggling in the water at a Hawaiian beach. The two psychologists contributed a set of science-based articles on what they called positive psychology in a special issue of *American Psychologist* in January of 2000.

In the years since their partnership began, they have created not only a science but also a movement determined to refocus American psychology on human strengths. It has attracted followers and fellow scientists from around the world. Positive psychology research has cataloged human strengths and virtues, which include wisdom, courage, kindness, and at least twenty-one others. It has studied creativity and exceptional talent and articulated what makes us happy, the power of optimism, and the qualities that define good work. It has also emphasized the need for civic virtues and healthy communities.

Situated historically, positive psychology owes much to earlier psychological research and practice. Looking to the future, it may help us adapt to a world of diminishing resources and increasing competition.

SEE ALSO Humanistic Psychology (1961), Black Psychology (1970), Flow: The Experience of Optimal Living (1990)

EMERGING ADULTHOOD

Jeffrey J. Arnett (b. 1955)

IN 1904, PSYCHOLOGIST G. STANLEY HALL argued that the physiological and psychological characteristics of individuals in their teen years were unique, and thus they should be considered as in a distinct life stage: adolescence. A half century later, psychologist Erik Erikson stated that adolescence was best characterized by the psychosocial challenge of forming a personal identity that would prepare an individual for the adult challenges of intimacy and vocational choice.

By the late twentieth century, some social scientists in developed, affluent countries began to notice that the path of young adults was not following the markers suggested by Hall and Erikson; they seemed to be in a transitional state that retained some of the traits of adolescence, such as identity formation, while also obtaining some adult characteristics, such as becoming sexually active, though typically without being married.

Jeffrey Arnett, a psychologist at Clark University (where, coincidentally, Hall had been the first president), began studying early adulthood in the 1990s. He decided that the label of "young adult" was inaccurate. It implied that adulthood had been reached even though many of the decisions and life choices that were typically thought to mark adulthood had not been made. He coined the term emerging adulthood to describe what he called a new life stage and fully described it in his 2004 book, *Emerging Adulthood*.

Individuals in the emerging-adulthood stage are best described as still in the process of forming a personal identity and choosing a vocation, often through higher education. Unlike the same age group fifty years earlier, they are less likely to be married or to have children. In the United States, more than 80 percent of individuals in emerging adulthood are sexually active, and more than half are in intimate, cohabiting relationships.

Jeffrey Arnett coined the term *emerging adulthood* to describe the period of life after adolescence, when many individuals in wealthy nations have graduated from high school but are still seeking an identity before committing to a vocation or life partner.

SEE ALSO Cultural Relativism: Culture, Sex, and Coming of Age (1928), Identity Crisis (1950)

DIAMOND'S *SEXUAL FLUIDITY*

Lisa Diamond (b. 1971)

Love Inspiring Sappho to Write an Ode to Music, by Francesco Bartolozzi, 1780. Sappho, the famous ancient Greek lyric poet, is widely known for her writing, as well as her bisexuality; the word *lesbian* is derived from her birthplace of Lesbos, an island in the Aegean Sea.

IF ANN COMES OUT AS A LESBIAN at age eighteen, does that prove her sexual orientation is fixed for the rest of her life? Will she always and only be attracted to other women? For many years the gay community has argued for a fixed-identity model of sexual attraction that is rooted in biology and thus not mutable. Such a model would posit that Ann has now settled forever on her sexual orientation.

In 2008, psychologist Lisa Diamond disturbed the status quo. In a series of articles, and in her subsequent book *Sexual Fluidity*, Diamond reported on her longitudinal study of seventy-nine lesbian, bisexual, and unlabeled women. Rather than a fixed identity, about two-thirds of the sample changed their sexual identification over the term of the study, and Diamond concluded that the most notable marker of women's sexual attraction is variability and change over time. Thus for women, more so than men, sexual identity is the result of the intersection of biology, environment, time, and context. Many of the women in her study reported it was the relationship that was important in the attraction.

In accord with this, Diamond has posited that sexual identity is a developmental process. When a person first recognizes a same-sex attraction, it is typically a very important moment. But with the passage of time, the person ceases to worry about sexual identity, and the focus shifts to relationship building.

It is this variability that Diamond refers to as sexual fluidity. She argues that for women, sexual orientation is not like a fixed compass point; in fact, there may not be a compass at all. Diamond now suggests that a better term to describe those for whom sexual attraction shifts over time is nonexclusive attraction. Her publications have triggered an enormous body of research on women's sexuality, now examined through the new lens of fluidity.

SEE ALSO Masters and Johnson's *Human Sexual Response* (1966), Beyond the Gender Binary (2017)

THE BRAIN INITIATIVE

Barack Obama (b. 1961)

ON APRIL 2, 2013, President Barack Obama announced the BRAIN Initiative. BRAIN is an acronym for Brain Research through Advancing Innovative Neurotechnologies, a new endeavor intended to dramatically expand the scientific understanding of the brain. The president and the scientists who planned the program hope that the resulting research will provide not only a deep insight into the basic science of brain function, but also new and better ways to treat, cure, and prevent brain disorders, including Alzheimer's disease and traumatic brain injury.

> BRAIN is an ambitious effort to map the activity of the brain while it is occurring.

The initiative is funded by a significant amount of federal funds ($100 million) channeled through three federal agencies: the National Institutes of Health (NIH), the Defense Advanced Research Projects Agency (DARPA), and the National Science Foundation (NSF). Private foundations also play a major role in funding the initiative, including the Allen Institute for Brain Science, the Howard Hughes Medical Institute, the Salk Institute for Biological Studies, and the Kavli Foundation.

BRAIN is an ambitious effort to map the activity of the brain while it is occurring; in fact, during the planning stages the project was called the Brain Activity Map. At the time of the announcement in 2013, scientists had the ability to record the communications of a few hundred neurons at a time. But the goal of the project is to map and record hundreds of thousands of brain cells while they are communicating with each other.

Already, initiative-funded research is making it possible to capture real-time pictures of complex neural circuits at the speed of thought. The goal is to create applications that directly link brain function and specific human behavior and learning, with the result that interventions for some of our most urgent brain diseases can be formulated. As of 2020, research funded by the initiative has shed light on the role of neural circuits in a range of key areas. For example, BRAIN-funded scientists have developed an objective measure of pain that is beginning to reveal how high-order brain circuits give rise to the experience of pain. This research may lead to more effective therapies in the treatment of pain.

The project is already generating new technologies and techniques, many of which are occurring via interdisciplinary collaborations among mathematicians, computer scientists, geneticists, molecular biologists, and scientists from multiple other fields.

SEE ALSO Where Brain Functions Are Localized (1861), Seeing the Brain at Work (1924)

BLACK LIVES MATTER

Patrisse Cullors (b. 1983), Alicia Garza (b. 1981), Opal Tometi (b. 1984)

IN 2014, AN EMERGENT BLACK ACTIVISM coalesced into a national and then international movement to challenge the ongoing violence and systemic racism directed against Black people. The phrase "Black Lives Matter" was first used in 2013 to call attention to racism and sanctioned violence against Black people after the acquittal of the killer of a young Black male named Trayvon Martin in February 2012. The term then was used in 2014 to identify an organized effort to protest the killings by police of Michael Brown in Ferguson, Missouri, and Eric Garner in Staten Island, NY. The leaders of Black Lives Matter expanded the movement across the country and then globally over the next few years as the systemic violence continued.

The movement is a contemporary response to long-standing institutional and systemic racism against marginalized communities. Historically, Black Lives Matter is linked to the protests of the Civil Rights movement of the 1950s and 1960s led by Martin Luther King Jr., and the Black nationalist/Black Power movement of the 1960s and 1970s inspired by Malcolm X.

The Civil Rights and Black Power movements deeply influenced a new cohort of African American psychologists to counter the scientific racism of white mainstream psychology. One of them, Dr. Joseph White, coined the term Black psychology to indicate a psychology based in the strengths of Black communities. Over time, their efforts changed the texture and emphases of American psychology, preparing the way for Black Lives Matter to have a major impact on psychology.

Since the formation of the movement, many psychologists have learned from the movement to think ecologically so that the collective, the interpersonal, and the intrapersonal needs of lives are addressed. It is a landmark

A Black Lives Matter protest in Philadelphia, on June 6, 2020, attended by more than 50,000 people. The protests led to the largest social movement in US history, with close to 30 million participants as of this writing, as well as protests across the world.

move to have psychological professions think beyond the individual to see and embrace others as full participants in the social, relational, and interior dimensions of life. After the killing by police of Breonna Taylor in Louisville, Kentucky, in March 2020 and George Floyd in Minneapolis, Minnesota, in May 2020, massive protests against anti-Black racism broke out across North America and elsewhere around the world. The protests led to the largest social movement in US history, with close to 30 million participants as of this writing.

SEE ALSO Contact Hypothesis or How to Reduce Racism and Bias (1954), Martin Luther King Jr., Psychology, and Social Justice (1967), Stereotype Threat (1995)

BEYOND THE GENDER BINARY

Kate Bornstein (b. 1948),
Stephanie Budge (b. 1982),
Judith Butler (b. 1956)

WHAT IS GENDER IDENTITY and what does it mean to think beyond a gender binary? Is the concept of gender necessary? There are ancient languages that have no word for *gender*. In the twentieth century, psychologists said that gender identity is the subjective sense a person has of his or her own masculinity or femininity and that it is independent of biological sex. One could experience gender identity disorder in which a person experiences significant psychological distress because they feel that their gender identity and biological sex are not aligned. This became a controversial and disputed disorder because it pathologized gender-nonconforming individuals.

Times have changed. In the twenty-first century, millions of children are growing up with an awareness that there is more to gender identity than the binary of masculine and feminine. Gender, rather, is best conceptualized as occurring on a continuum or falling on a spectrum of gender identities. One can be *genderfluid*, that is, a person whose gender identity or expression may shift between masculine and feminine or even fall somewhere along the spectrum. A person may have an identity of nonbinary, rejecting an either/or categorization and identifying, among many possibilities, as *agender* or *genderqueer* or *transgender*. Many who reject the gender binary choose pronouns that they feel best suit them or use original pronouns.

The emergence of so many diverse expressions and identities is not restricted to North America or the Western world. Surveys have found that more than half of the teenagers surveyed believe that gender is a spectrum and not a binary. Indeed, in some societies, there are long-established gender identities that are neither masculine nor feminine. It may help if we see this movement beyond a gender binary as a step toward greater freedom, as social science research has found that where gender roles are distinctive and enforced, there is more violence and greater inequality.

> Gender . . . is best conceptualized as occurring on a continuum or falling on a spectrum of gender identities.

Philosopher Judith Butler's 1990 book *Gender Trouble* is often characterized as a key text for creating an understanding of gender as a performance and not as an essential identity. Gender is performed, she argues, through speech, actions, dress, and behavior. The book and related articles served to give a language to the nonbinary gender experience. Kate Bornstein was assigned a male gender at birth, but came to the realization that being male was only a performance. After gender reassignment surgery, they experienced the same sense of performance. They chose a nonbinary gender identity. Through their work as a playwright, performance artist, and gender theorist, Bornstein has been a model and an advocate for lives beyond the gender binary. Stephanie Budge is a counseling psychologist who has studied coping processes in transgender individuals with an accompanying focus on effective treatments. She and her colleagues have found that nonbinary people make up a large portion of the transgender population. Nonbinary individuals are at greater risk of suicide and often experience high levels of depression and anxiety.

SEE ALSO Masters and Johnson's *Human Sexual Response* (1966), Diamond's *Sexual Fluidity* (2008)

2019

TRADITIONAL KNOWLEDGE—
INDIGENOUS PSYCHOLOGIES

Virgilio Enriquez (1942–94), Ignacio Martín-Baró (1942–89), Durganand Sinha (1922–98)

THE UNITED NATIONS (UN) declared 2019 the Year of Traditional Knowledge. Such knowledge, or knowledges, are the basis of indigenous people's identities, culture, sustenance, and coping. For indigenous societies, these bodies of knowledge reflect centuries or even millennia of learning how to best live in unique environments. Not only are the knowledges

sources of practical guidance, they also draw on and inform cultural rituals and spiritual practices. Traditional knowledges are the foundations of the world's cultural diversity and for managing global biodiversity. Indigenous peoples' skill in managing biodiversity and living sustainably on their land is crucial now and for humanity's future.

Traditional knowledges are also critical resources for indigenous psychologies. The development of indigenous psychologies as an alternative to Western psychology began in the mid-twentieth century when psychology as the study of the individual was introduced by Westerners. What happened in many cultures was the discovery that Western psychology did not fit well with local traditional knowledge and society. Many societies were and are based on group or collective identity and have an expectation that being a person is based on the relationships that one has, whether in families, tribes, or larger social units. In more traditional societies, the core relationship for everyone is with the earth and the natural world.

Indigenous psychologies have now developed in many cultures around the world. Some, as in China, seek to develop a psychology that accords with Western psychology but that draws on local cultural norms. Other indigenous psychologies, such as Sikolohiyang Pilipino, have developed research methods based in traditional and cultural knowledge. Still others, especially among indigenous peoples, do not divide knowledge into categories such as psychology or sociology. Rather, their psychology is part of their connection with the earth and with each other and informs their understanding of life in every dimension. Almost certainly, the future of psychology is tied to the development of indigenous psychologies.

OPPOSITE: Different types of indigenous psychologies have developed in many cultures around the world. Here, community members in a Philippine village help move a house to a new location—a volunteerism tradition still practiced today. The image illustrates the close connection between culture and psychological constructs that are part of Sikolohiyang Pilipino.

SEE ALSO Nurturant-Task Model of Leadership (1980), Sikolohiyang Pilipino (1975), Social Ontogenesis: Culture and Development in Africa (1992)

CLIMATE CRISIS PSYCHOLOGY

Thomas Berry (1914–2009), Joanna Macy (b. 1929),
Andy Fisher (b. 1963), Wade Pickren (b. 1952),
Linda Weintraub (b. 1942)

BY 2020 IT WAS OBVIOUS that human behavior had precipitated a climate crisis of global reach. As early as the 1970s, environmental thinkers like Thomas Berry and Joanna Macy had begun to articulate a Great Transition to values and actions that would bring humans into partnership with the earth. This meant re-centering the "good life" from consumption and endless economic growth to values of the connectedness of all things, preservation of cultural and bio-diversity, and acceptance that we live in a sentient universe where consciousness is characteristic of all beings.

> We need a new orientation that places the earth first and asks of humans to learn to think and feel with the earth.

Psychologist Theodore Roszak offered an early ecopsychology in the 1970s. In his book, *Radical Ecopsychology* (2002, 2013), Andy Fisher brought clarity to the need for an ecopsychology that recognizes its dependence on and connection with the earth and that does not view humans as privileged members of life on earth.

This author built on Roszak's and Fisher's work to develop a psychology suitable to meet the intertwining crises of climate change, massive biodiversity loss, and rising social inequality. Believing that a climate crisis psychology must be informed by the arts, I partnered with artist-scholar Linda

Weintraub, who developed eco materialism to acknowledge the emotional and cognitive effects of environmental collapse. Our exploration relates the physical state of planet Earth to contemporary art, contemporary philosophy, and contemporary lifestyles. All derive from contemporary human mindsets, which form the psychology connection.

I challenged psychology to move beyond its narrow focus on individual responsibility, which is inadequate to address the climate crisis and the cognate crises that are related, such as the Covid-19 crisis that began in 2020. Scientists have shown that viral pandemics are increasingly connected to the intrusion of humans into wildlife habitats and to increased air pollution. I argued that we need a new orientation that places the earth first and asks of humans to learn to think and feel with the earth, an approach long practiced by many indigenous peoples. A psychology based on this orientation and drawing on the creative power of the arts will make possible a regenerative psychology marked by relationality, reciprocity, and resilience. Such a psychology is needed for our climate crisis.

SEE ALSO Bees Dancing, Egg-Rolling Birds, and the New Science of Ethology (1952), Traditional Knowledge—Indigenous Psychologies (2019)

Further Reading and Sources

General Reading

Baker, D. B. (ed.), *Oxford Handbook of the History of Psychology: Global Perspectives*. New York: Oxford, 2012.

Fancher, R. E. & Rutherford, A., *Pioneers of Psychology* (4th Edition). New York: Norton, 2012.

Ferngren, G. B., *The History of Science and Religion in the Western Tradition*. New York: Garland, 2000.

Freedheim, D. K. (ed.), *Handbook of Psychology. Volume 1: History of Psychology* (2nd ed). New York: Wiley, 2013.

Grob, G. N., *The Mad Among Us: A History of the Care of America's Mentally Ill*. New York: Free Press, 1994.

Mazlish, B., *The Uncertain Sciences*. New York: Transaction, 2007.

Mitchell, S. A., & Black, M. J., *Freud and Beyond: A History of Modern Psychoanalytic Thought*. New York: Basic Books, 1996.

Porter, R., *The Greatest Benefit to Mankind*. New York: Norton, 1997.

Rao, K. R., Paranjpe, A. C., & Dalal, A. K. (Eds.), *Handbook of Indian Psychology*. New Delhi: Foundation, 2008.

Shorter, E., *A History of Psychiatry*. New York: Wiley, 1997.

Smith, R., *Norton History of the Human Sciences*. New York: Norton, 1997.

———, *Between Mind and Nature: A History of Psychology*. London: Reaktion Books, 2013.

Sources

c. 10,000 BCE / Shamanism: Kakar, S., *Shamans, Mystics and Doctors: A Psychological Inquiry into India and its Healing Traditions*. Chicago: Univ. of Chicago Press, 1991; Ellenberger, H. F., *The Discovery of the Unconscious*. New York: Basic Books, 1970.

528 BCE / Buddha's Four Noble Truths: Mishra, P., *An End to Suffering: The Buddha in the World*. New York: Picador, 2005.

c. 500 BCE / Confucian Psychology: Bond, M. H., *Oxford Handbook of Chinese Psychology*. New York: Oxford Univ. Press, 2010.

c. 350 BCE / Asclepius and the Art of Healing: Porter, T., *The Greatest Benefit to Mankind: A Medical History of Humanity*. New York: Norton, 1999.

c. 200 BCE / Bhagavad Gita: Doniger, W., *The Hindus: An Alternative History*. New York: Penguin, 2010.

c. 160 CE / Humoral Theory: Porter, T., *The Greatest Benefit to Mankind: A Medical History of Humanity*. New York: Norton, 1999.

1025 / Avicenna and the First Islamic Psychology: Nasr, S. H., & Leaman, O. (Eds.), *History of Islamic Philosophy*. New York: Routledge, 2001.

1517 / Protestantism and the Psychological Self: Taylor, C., *Sources of the Self: The Making of the Modern Identity*. Cambridge, MA: Harvard Univ. Press, 1992.

1580 / Montaigne's *Essays*: Bakewell, S., *How to Live: Or A Life of Montaigne in One Question and Twenty Attempts at an Answer*. New York: Other Press, 2010.

1637 / Descartes on Mind and Body: Smith, R., *The Norton History of the Human Sciences*. New York: Norton, 1997.

1664 / *Cerebri Anatome*: On the Brain and Behavior: Richards, G., *Mental Machinery: Origins and Consequences of Psychological Ideas from 1600–1850*. Amherst, NY: Prometheus Books, 1992.

1690 / Tabula Rasa: The Psychology of Experience: Smith, R., *The Norton History of the Human Sciences*. New York: Norton, 1997.

1762 / Rousseau's Natural Child: Porter, R., *The Enlightenment*. New York: Palgrave Macmillan, 2001.

1766 / Mesmerism: Lamont, P., *Extraordinary Beliefs: A Historical Approach to a Psychological Problem*. New York: Cambridge Univ. Press, 2013.

1832 / Phrenology: Stern, M., *Heads & Headlines: The Phrenological Fowlers*. Norman, OK: Univ. of Oklahoma Press, 1971.

1834 / Fechner and the Just-Noticeable Difference (JND): Heidelberger, M., *Nature from Within: Gustav Theodor Fechner and his Psychophysical Worldview*. Pittsburgh, PA: Univ. of Pittsburgh Press, 2004.

1843 / The First Thinking Machine: Woolley, B., *The Bride of Science: Romance, Reason, and Byron's Daughter*. New York: McGraw-Hill, 1999.

1848 / The Curious Case of Phineas Gage: Macmillan, M., *An Odd Kind of Fame: Stories of Phineas Gage*. Cambridge, MA: Bradford Books, 2002.

1851 / Bipolar Disorder and Creativity: Jamison, K. R., *Touched with Fire: Manic-Depressive Illness and the Artistic Temperament*. New York: Free Press, 1993.

1859 / Darwin's *On the Origin of Species*: Browne, J., *Darwin's Origin of Species: A Biography*. London: Atlantic Books, 2006.

1859 / Mind-Cure: Taylor, E., *Shadow Culture: Psychology and Spirituality in America*. Washington, DC: Counterpoint, 1999.

1861 / Where Brain Functions Are Localized: Young, R. M., *Mind, Brain, and Adaptation in the*

Nineteenth Century: Cerebral Localization and Its Biological Context from Gall to Ferrier. New York: Oxford, 1990.

1867 / Prosopagnosia: The Inability to Recognize Faces: Sacks, O., *The Man Who Mistook His Wife For A Hat: And Other Clinical Tales.* New York: Touchstone, 1985.

1871 / Synesthesia: Numbers as Colors or Tuesday Is Red: Cytowic, R. E., *The Man Who Tasted Shapes.* Cambridge, MA: MIT Press, 2003.

1874 / Nature vs. Nurture: Segal, N. L., *Born Together–Reared Apart: The Landmark Minnesota Twin Study.* Cambridge, MA: Harvard Univ. Press, 2012.

1874 / Psychology Becomes a Science: Goodwin, C. J., *A History of Modern Psychology* (4th ed.). New York: Wiley, 2011.

1880 / Anna O.: Converting Psychological Distress into Physical Illness: Kimball, M. M. (2000), "From Anna O. to Bertha Pappenheim: Transforming Private Pain into Public Action." *History of Psychology*, 3: 20–43.

1885 / Multiple Personality Disorder: Hacking, I., *Rewriting the Soul: Multiple Personality and the Sciences of Memory.* Princeton, NJ: Princeton Univ. Press, 1995.

1886 / *Psychopathia Sexualis*: Bullough, V. L., *Science in the Bedroom: A History of Sex Research.* New York: Basic Books, 1995.

1890 / James's *The Principles of Psychology*: Menand, L., *The Metaphysical Club.* New York: Farrar, Straus, and Giroux, 2002; Richardson, R. D., *William James: In the Maelstrom of American Modernism.* New York: Mariner, 2007.

1898 / Western Cultural Bias: The Torres Straits Expedition: Herle, A. & Rouse, S., *Cambridge and the Torres Strait.* London: Cambridge Univ. Press, 1998.

1899 / Psychoanalysis: The Talking Cure: Fine, R., *The History of Psychoanalysis. New Expanded Edition.* Northvale: Jason Aronson, 1979.

1900 / *The Interpretation of Dreams* **Inaugurates the Century of Psychology:** Freud, S., & Brill, A. A., *The Basic Writings of Sigmund Freud.* New York: Modern Library, 1995. This volume contains *The Interpretation of Dreams*, and no one is better to read on the topic than Freud himself.

1902 / Forensic Psychology: Loftus, E. R., *Eyewitness Testimony.* Cambridge, MA: Harvard Univ. Press, 1996.

1903 / Classical Conditioning: Pavlov's Bell: Todes, D., *Pavlov's Physiology Factory: Experiment, Interpretation, Laboratory Enterprise.* Baltimore: Johns Hopkins, 2001.

1904 / Culture Determines What Counts as Mental Illness: Kleinman, A., *Patients and Healers in the Context of Culture.* Berkeley, CA: Univ. of California Press, 1981.

1905 / Binet and Simon: The First Intelligence Test: Wolf, T. H., *Alfred Binet.* Chicago: Univ. of Chicago Press, 1973.

1908 / Bleuler Initiates the Modern Study of the Schizophrenias: Green, M. F., *Schizophrenia Revealed: From Neurons to Social Interactions.* New York: Norton, 2003.

1909 / Can Apes Learn Human Language?: Savage-Rumbaugh, S., & Lewin, R., *Kanzi: The Ape at the Brink of the Human Mind.* New York: Wiley, 1996.

1912 / Gestalt Psychology: The Whole Is Greater than the Sum of Its Parts: Ash, M. G., *Gestalt Psychology in German Culture, 1890–1967: Holism and the Quest for Objectivity.* New York: Cambridge Univ. Press, 1995.

1912 / Experimental Neurosis: How Animals Can Be Made Crazy: Liddell, H. S., *Emotional Hazards in Animals and Man.* Springfield, IL: Charles Thomas, 1956.

1913 / Jungian Psychology: Collective Unconscious and Psychological Growth: Jung, C. G. (Trans.: S. Shamdasani, M. Kyburz, & J. Peck), *The Red Book.* New York: Norton, 2009.

1913 / The Lie Detector and the Golden Lasso of Truth: Bunn, G., *The Truth Machine: A Social History of the Lie Detector.* Baltimore, MD: Johns Hopkins, 2012.

1914 / Variability Hypothesis: Gender and Genius: Haraway, D., *Primate Visions: Gender, Race, and Nature in the World of Modern Science.* New York: Routledge, 1989; Shields, S. A. (1982), "The Variability Hypothesis: The History of a Biological Model of Sex Differences in Intelligence," *Signs*, 7: 769–97.

1915 / Transforming Western Psychology in India: Sinha, D., *Psychology in a Third World Country: The Indian Experience.* Delhi: Sage, 1986.

1921 / Army Intelligence Tests and Scientific Racism: Sokal, M. M. (ed.), *Psychological Testing and American Society, 1890–1930.* New Brunswick, NJ: Rutgers Univ. Press, 1987.

1921 / Projective Tests: The Rorschach Inkblots: Butcher, J. N. (2010), "Personality Assessment from the Nineteenth to the Early Twenty-First Century: Past Achievements and Contemporary Challenges." *Annual Review of Clinical Psychology*, 6: 1–20.

1922 / Feminine Psychology: Horney, K., *Feminine Psychology.* New York: Norton, 1993.

1923 / Capgras Syndrome: Ramachandran, V. S. & Blakeslee, S., *Phantoms in the Brain: Probing the Mysteries of the Human Mind.* New York: William Morrow, 1998.

1924 / Seeing the Brain at Work: Dumit, J., *Picturing Personhood: Brain Scans and Biomedical Identity.*

Princeton, NJ: Princeton Univ. Press, 2004; Schoonover, C., *Portraits of the Mind: Visualizing the Brain from Antiquity to the 21st Century*. New York: Abrams, 2010.

1925 / Somatotypes: Does Body Shape Reflect our Personality?: Sheldon, W., *Atlas of Men: A Guide for Somatotyping the Adult Image of All Ages*. New York: Macmillan, 1970.

1928 / Cultural Relativism: Culture, Sex, and Coming of Age: Lutkehaus, N., *Margaret Mead: The Making of an American Icon*. Princeton, NJ: Princeton Univ. Press, 2008.

1930 / The Skinner Chamber: Rutherford, A., *Beyond the Box: B. F. Skinner's Technology of Behavior from Laboratory to Life, 1950s–1970s*. Toronto: Univ. of Toronto Press, 2009.

1932 / Remembering and Forgetting: Bartlett, F. C., *Remembering: A Study in Experimental and Social Psychology*. Cambridge, UK: Cambridge Univ. Press, 1932.

1934 / Archetypes: Trickster, Sage, Hero, and Primordial Mother: Shamdasani, S., *Jung and the Making of Modern Psychology: The Dream of a Science*. New York: Cambridge Univ. Press, 2003.

1934 / Zone of Proximal Development: Mooney, C. G., *Theories of Childhood: An Introduction to Dewey, Montessori, Erikson, Piaget & Vygotsky*. St. Paul, MN: Redleaf, 2000.

1935 / Thematic Apperception Test: Our Stories and Our Personality: Robinson, F., *Love's Story Told: A Biography of Henry Murray*. Cambridge, MA: Harvard Univ. Press, 1992.

1935 / Psychosurgery: Pressman, J. D., *Last Resort: Psychosurgery and the Limits of Medicine*. New York: Cambridge Univ. Press, 1998.

1936 / Defense Mechanisms: Freud, A., *The Ego and the Mechanisms of Defense*. New York: International Universities Press, 1936/1979.

1937 / Turing Machine: Leavitt, D., *The Man Who Knew Too Much: Alan Turing and the Invention of the Computer*. New York: Norton, 2006.

1941 / Direct Brain Stimulation and Experiential Hallucinations: Penfield, W., *The Mystery of the Mind: A Critical Study of Consciousness and the Human Brain*. Princeton, NJ: Princeton Univ. Press, 1975.

1943 / Cybernetics, Computers, and the Beginning of Cognitive Science: Gardner, H., *The Mind's New Science: A History of the Cognitive Revolution*. New York: Basic Books, 1987.

1943 / The Doll Studies: Racism and Child Self-Image: Markowitz, G., & Rosner, D., *Children, Race, and Power: Kenneth and Mamie Clark's Northside Center*. New York: Routledge, 2000.

1943 / Maslow Creates the Hierarchy of Needs: Maslow, A. H., *Motivation and Personality* (2nd ed.). New York: Harper & Row, 1954/1970.

1943 / Autism: Grandin, T., *The Way I See It, Revised and Expanded 2nd Edition: A Personal Look at Autism and Asperger's*. Arlington, TX: Future Horizons, 2011.

1944 / Sex Roles: Broverman, I. K., Vogel, S. R., Broverman, D. M., Clarkson, F. E., & Rosenkrantz, P. S. (1972), "Sex Role Stereotypes: A Current Appraisal," *The Journal of Social Issues*, 28: 59–78; Unger, R. K., *Resisting Gender: Twenty-five Years of Feminist Psychology*. London: Sage, 1998.

1946 / Logotherapy and the Search for Meaning: Frankl, V., *Man's Search for Meaning*. New York: Washington Square, 1962.

1947 / Rogers's Client-Centered Therapy: Rogers, C., *On Becoming a Person: A Therapist's View of Psychotherapy*. London: Constable, 1961.

1948 / Neuroplasticity: Ramachandran, V. S., *The Tell-Tale Brain: A Neuroscientist's Quest for What Makes Us Human*. New York: Norton, 2012.

1950 / The Discovery of Stress: Becker, D., *One Nation Under Stress: The Trouble with Stress as an Idea*. New York: Oxford Univ. Press, 2013; Cooper, C. L., & Dewe, P. J., *Stress: A Brief History*. New York: Wiley-Blackwell, 2004.

1950 / Identity Crisis: Erikson, E., *Childhood and Society*. New York: Norton, 1950/1993.

1951 / Conformity and Independence: Greenwood, J. D., *The Disappearance of the Social in American Social Psychology*. New York: Cambridge Univ. Press, 2004.

1952 / Bees Dancing, Egg-Rolling Birds, and the New Science of Ethology: Vicedo, M., *The Nature and Nurture of Love: From Imprinting to Attachment in Cold War America*. Chicago: Univ. of Chicago Press, 2013.

1952 / *Lives in Progress*: Psychology and the Story of Our Lives: White, R. W., *Lives in Progress: A Study of the Natural Growth in Personality*. New York: Holt, Rinehart, & Winston, 1952, 1966, 1975.

1953 / The Case of H. M.: Hilts, P. J., *Memory's Ghost: The Nature of Memory and the Strange Tale of Mr. M.* New York: Simon & Schuster, 1996.

1953 / REM and the Cycles of Sleep: Hobson, A., *Dreaming: A Very Short Introduction*. New York: Oxford Univ. Press, 2011.

1954 / Pleasure and Pain Centers: Olds, J. (1956), "Pleasure Center in the Brain." *Scientific American*, 195: 105–16.

1954 / Contact Hypothesis or How to Reduce Racism and Bias: Allport, G., *The Nature of Prejudice*. New York: Basic Books, 1954/1979.

1955 / Cognitive Therapy: Beck, A. T., Rush, A. J., Shaw, B. F., Emery, G., *Cognitive Therapy of Depression*. New York: Guilford Press, 1979; Ellis, A., *A Guide to Rational Living*. Englewood Cliffs, NJ: Prentice-Hall, 1961.

1955 / Placebo Effect: Harrington, A., *The Cure Within: A History of Mind-Body Medicine*. New York: Norton, 2008.

1957 / Antidepressant Medications: Healy, D., *The Anti-Depressant Era*. Cambridge, MA: Harvard Univ. Press, 1999.

1957 / Cognitive Dissonance: How Humans Maintain Psychological Consistency: Tavris, C., & Aronson, E., *Mistakes Were Made (But Not by Me): Why We Justify Foolish Beliefs, Bad Decisions, and Hurtful Acts*. New York: Mariner Books, 2008.

1957 / Hooker's Research: Homosexuality Is Not an Illness: Minton, H. L., *Departing from Deviance: A History of Homosexual Rights and Emancipatory Science in America*. Chicago: Univ. of Chicago Press, 2001.

1958 / Mother Love: Vicedo, M., *The Nature and Nurture of Love: From Imprinting to Attachment in Cold War America*. Chicago: Univ. of Chicago Press, 2013.

1959 / Type A Personality: Friedman, M., *Treating Type A Behavior—And Your Heart*. New York: Fawcett, 1985.

1960 / The Visual Cliff: Gibson, E. J., & Walk, R. D. (Apr. 1960), "The Visual Cliff." *Scientific American*, 202: 64–71.

1961 / Humanistic Psychology: Grogan, J., *Encountering America: Humanistic Psychology, Sixties Culture, and the Shaping of the Modern Self*. New York: Harper, 2012.

1962 / Right Brain, Left Brain: Rose, N., & Abi-Rached, J. M., *Neuro: The New Brain Sciences and the Management of the Mind*. Princeton, NJ: Princeton Univ. Press, 2013.

1963 / Friedan's *The Feminine Mystique*: Friedan, B., *The Feminine Mystique*. New York: Norton, 1963; Coontz, S., *A Strange Stirring: The Feminine Mystique and American Women at the Dawn of the 1960s*. New York: Basic Books, 2011.

1963 / Milgram's Obedience Experiments: Blass, T., *The Man Who Shocked the World: The Life and Legacy of Stanley Milgram*. New York: Basic Books, 2004.

1965 / Head Start: Zigler, E., & Muenchow, S., *Head Start: The Inside Story of America's Most Successful Educational Experiment*. New York: Basic Books, 1994.

1966 / Masters and Johnson's *Human Sexual Response*: Masters, W. H. & Johnson, V. E., *Human Sexual Response*. Boston: Little Brown, 1966.

1967 / Martin Luther King Jr., Psychology, and Social Justice: King Jr., M. L. (1968), "The Role of the Behavioral Scientist in the Civil Rights Movement." *American Psychologist*, 23: 180–86.

1969 / Attachment Theory: Bowlby, J., *Attachment and Loss*. New York: Basic Books, 1969; Vicedo, M., *The Nature and Nurture of Love: From Imprinting to Attachment in Cold War America*. Chicago: Univ. of Chicago Press, 2013.

1969 / Five Stages of Grief: Kübler-Ross, E., *On Death and Dying*. New York: Routledge, 1969.

1970 / Black Psychology: Guthrie, R. V., *Even the Rat Was White* (2nd ed.). Boston: Allyn & Bacon, 1998.

1970 / The BITCH Test: Williams, R. L., *History of the Association of Black Psychologists*. Bloomington, IN: Author-House, 2008.

1971 / Stanford Prison Experiment: Zimbardo, P., *The Lucifer Effect: Understanding How Good People Turn Evil*. New York: Random House, 2008.

1973 / Resilience: Werner, E. E. & Smith, R. S., *Overcoming the Odds: High Risk Children from Birth to Adulthood*. Ithaca, NY: Cornell Univ. Press, 1992.

1974 / Judgment Under Uncertainty: Kahneman, D., *Thinking Fast and Slow*. New York: Farrar, Straus, & Giroux, 2013.

1975 / Psychoneuroimmunology: Sternberg, E. S., *The Balance Within: The Science Connecting Health and Emotions*. New York: Freeman, 2001.

1975 / Sikolohiyang Pilipino: Enriquez, V., "Developing a Filipino Psychology." In U. Kim & J. W. Berry (Eds.), *Indigenous Psychologies* (152–69). Newbury Park, CA: Sage, 1993.

1978 / Theory of Mind: Tomasello, M., *The Cultural Origins of Human Cognition*. Cambridge, Harvard Univ. Press, 1999.

1979 / Ecological Systems Theory: Rogoff, B., *The Cultural Nature of Human Development*. New York: Oxford Univ. Press, 2003.

1979 / Social Identity Theory: Tajfel, Henri, *Differentiation between Social Groups: Studies in the Social Psychology of Intergroup Relations*. London and New York: Academic Press, 1978.

1980 / Nurturant-Task Model of Leadership: Budhwar, P. S., & Varma, A., *Doing Business in India*. New York: Routledge, 2010.

1980 / Post-Traumatic Stress Disorder (PTSD): Young, A., *The Harmony of Illusions: Inventing Post-Traumatic Stress Disorder*. Princeton, NJ: Princeton Univ. Press, 1997.

1983 / Multiple Intelligences: Gardner, H., *Multiple Intelligences: New Horizons in Theory and Practice*. New York: Basic Books, 2006.

1989 / Liberation Psychology: Martín-Baró, I., *Writings for a Liberation Psychology*. Cambridge, MA: Harvard Univ. Press, 1996.

1990 / Flow: The Experience of Optimal Living: Csikszentmihalyi, M., *Flow*. New York: Harper and Row, 1990.

1992 / Mirror Neurons: Iacoboni, M., *Mirroring People: The New Science of How We Connect with Others.*

1992 / Social Ontogenesis: Nsamenang, A. B., *Human Development in Cultural Context: A Third World Perspective.* Newbury Park, CA: Sage, 1992.

1993 / Mindfulness and Mind-Body Medicine—Body Medicine: Moyers, B., *Healing and the Mind.* New York: Doubleday, 1995.

1995 / Looping Effects of Human Kinds: Hacking, I., "The Looping Effects of Human Kinds." In D. Sperber, D. Premack, and A. Premack (Eds.), *Causal Cognition: An Interdisciplinary Approach* (pp. 351–383). Oxford: Oxford Univ. Press, 1995; Hacking, I., *Historical Ontology.* Cambridge, MA: Harvard Univ. Press, 2002.

1995 / Stereotype Threat: Steele, C. M., & Aronson, J. (1995), "Stereotype Threat and the Intellectual Test Performance of African Americans." *Journal of Personality and Social Psychology*, 69: 797–811.

1996 / Autonomous-Relational Self: Kagitçibasi, Ç. (1996), "The autonomous-relational self: A new synthesis." *European Psychologist*, 1: 180–86.

2000 / Positive Psychology: Snyder, C. R. & Lopez, S. J. (Eds.) *Handbook of Positive Psychology.* New York: Oxford Univ. Press, 2002.

2004 / Emerging Adulthood: Arnett, J. J. *Emerging Adulthood: The Winding Road from the Late Teens Through the Twenties.* Oxford: Oxford Univ. Press, 2004.

2008 / Diamond's *Sexual Fluidity*: Diamond, L., *Sexual Fluidity: Understanding Women's Love and Desire.* Cambridge, MA: Harvard Univ. Press, 2008.

2013 / The BRAIN Initiative: See http://www.nih.gov/science/brain/; Rose, N., & Abi-Rached, J. M., *Neuro: The New Brain Sciences and the Management of the Mind.* Princeton, NJ: Princeton Univ. Press, 2013.

2014 / Black Lives Matter: https://blacklivesmatter.com/herstory/; Chase, G. (2017–18), "The Early History of the Black Lives Matter Movement, and the Implications Thereof," *Nevada Law Journal*, 18: 1091–112.

2017 / Beyond the Gender Binary: Bornstein, K. *Gender Outlaw: On Men, Women, and the Rest of Us.* New York: Routledge, 1994; Butler, J. *Gender Trouble: Feminism and the Subversion of Identity.* New York, NY: Routledge, 1990; Matsuno, E. & Budge, S. L. (2017). "Non-binary/Genderqueer Identities: A Critical Review of the Literature, *Current Sexual Health Reports*, 9: 116–20; University of Wisconsin-Madison Trans Care Lab, Stephanie Budge: https://trl.education.wisc.edu/people/

2019 / Traditional Knowledge—Indigenous Psychologies: Enriquez, V. G., *Pagbabangong-Dangal: Indigenous Psychology and Cultural Empowerment.* Quezon City, Philippines: Akademya ng Kultura at Sikolohiyang Pilipino, 1994; Martín-Baró, I., *Writings for a Liberation Psychology.* Cambridge, MA: Harvard University Press, 1996; Sinha, D., *Psychology in a Third World Country: The Indian Experience.* Beverly Hills, CA: Sage, 1986; https://www.un.org/development/desa/indigenouspeoples/wp-content/uploads/sites/19/2019/04/Traditional-Knowledge-backgrounder-FINAL.pdf

2020 / Climate Crisis Psychology: Berry, T., *The Great Work: Our Way into the Future.* New York: Bell Tower, 1999; Fisher, A., *Radical Ecopsychology: Psychology in the Service of Life (2nd ed).* Albany, NY: SUNY, 2013; Macy, J., *World as Lover, World as Self: Courage for Global Justice and Ecological Renewal.* Berkeley, CA: Parallax, 2007; Pickren, W., (2020, May). "Psychologies Otherwise & Earthwise: Pluriversal Approaches to the Crises of Climate, Equity, and Health," keynote address, Conference on the Psychology of Global Crises: State Surveillance, Solidarity and Everyday Life, American University of Paris, May 20–30, 2020. To be published in 2021 In M. Dege (Ed.), *The Psychology of Global Crises and Crisis Politics: Intervention, Resistance, Decolonization.* New York: Palgrave; Weintraub, L., *To Life! Eco Art in Pursuit of a Sustainable Planet.* Berkeley, CA: University of California Press, 2012.

Index

Page numbers in *italics* include illustrations and photographs

Acknowledgments

I WOULD LIKE TO THANK the many scholars whose insightful work informed me as I wrote this book. Numerous historians of science, medicine, professional practice, and technology have shaped my thinking about the history of psychology. Members of Cheiron: The International Society for the History of Behavioral and Social Sciences as well as the Forum for History of Human Science and the Society for the History of Psychology all shed much-needed light on the many tributaries of thought and practice that have flowed together to create contemporary psychology. I thank the editorial team at Sterling, especially Barbara Berger, for all their help and wisdom; also thanks to Christine Heun for the beautiful interior design, Elizabeth Mihaltse Lindy for the stunning cover, and production editor Michael Cea—it has been a team effort. A very special thanks to Alexandra Rutherford, whose support and insight helped make it possible for me to complete this book.

Picture Credits